MEN'S KNITS

erika knight

MEN'SKNITS
20 New Classics

POTTER
CRAFT

New York

contents

BASICS 20

striped full-zip cardigan 22

week day sweater 28

1950s-style cardigan 32

half-zip sweater 38

casual cardigan 44

simple vest 50

hand-dyed sweater 58

multi-stripe sweater 62

favorite sweatshirt 68

herringbone sweater 74

collegiate cardigan 80

new classic v-neck and crewneck sweaters 90

fine-knit cardigan 96

plain, argyle, and checkered vests 102

funnel-neck sweater 110

cabled sweater 114

weekend hat 122

beanie 126

striped scarf 130

big cable scarf 134

introduction

Maybe growing up in a household with four brothers had some bearing on my lifelong passion for menswear. Inevitably I grew up a tomboy, often being put to use as one half of a goal post partnered by a divested sweater. I have always had a thing about knitwear, too. Perhaps that's partly down to such formative childhood experiences and partly down to my granny, of course. All the signs were there early on. Later in life, I shared my woolly ethos with my ex-Mod and sharp-dressing partner, Ian. With his keen eye for style and my passion for knits, we found a niche within the world of menswear and created our own label **Molto!** During the eighties, we designed and made unique hand knits for men that sold worldwide; iconic pieces worn by many "faces" of the era, perhaps most memorably by Boy George. Recommended to a top Italian designer, I learned my trade in Italy, working with patternmakers and technicians who had trained under the French mistress of couture, Coco Chanel herself. I was given carte blanche to design for a bigger international arena: I believe I learned all there is to know about creating the quintessential polo shirt.

In designing the garments for this book, it has been great putting together simple pieces that anyone can knit for a father, brother, husband, boyfriend, or friend, for him to style in his own way. I was taught in Italy that a sweater should be suitable for any man, whether he is 17 or 71, and so this is what I have set out to do. Whenever I am designing knitwear, I always follow the principle of leading British couturier Hardy Amies:

"Nowhere is design more important. Discard design and a knitted garment can quickly become dowdy, overdesign it and it becomes a mess; we are at our best working within such strict confines."

For me, the perfect sweater becomes an "old friend"; it is comfortable and familiar, worn and well traveled. A man's knit can be a piece for sharing—discretely borrowing it from the guy in your life—faintly imbued with his reassuring and evocative scent. It is a sexy thing to give the man in your life a sweater, soft and luxurious, revealing your nurturing, feminine side. I love authentic workwear, sportswear, military, and country clothing, all of which have inspired my designs over the years. I love the pragmatism and robustness of men's garments: overalls, fishing sweaters, Guernseys, and Arans all offer a wealth of resources for design and detail. So I have put together some good basic menswear shapes to knit time and time again. Alternatively, these designs could be used as a starting point to make him something a little bit unexpected, with a twist of individuality and some homemade attitude.

Within the pages of this book, I hope you find something to make for each of the boys in your life, or perhaps even for yourself.

Erika Knight

knitting know-how

TYPES OF YARN

I always choose to use authentic, natural fibers in my designs, derived from either animal or vegetable sources. Natural yarns tend to have unique properties that give each garment a strong character. For me, this is especially important when selecting yarns menswear. Natural yarns are distinctly individual; they allow the skin to breathe while providing ultimate comfort.

Alpaca

A pure, natural, and luxurious fiber to rival cashmere. With a beautiful drape, subtle sheen, and extreme softness, it glides through the fingers, making it a great choice for hand knitters. Alpaca comes in a large number of natural shades.

Due to its hollow fibers and microscopic air pockets, pure alpaca is completely thermal, retaining warmth whilst remaining breathable and absorbing moisture. Being naturally water- and dust-repellent, alpaca makes a great choice for sweaters, especially outdoor wear.

Bamboo

Bamboo yarn is derived from a grass that is harvested and distilled into cellulose, which is then spun into yarn. It is a renewable and sustainable resource and thrives with no need for any pesticides. It can be harvested without killing the plant, and it only takes a few months before the bamboo is ready to be harvested again. All this makes it a very eco-friendly yarn.

Pure bamboo fiber is biodegradable and naturally antibacterial. It is extremely cool to wear, taking moisture away from the skin and allowing it to breathe. Bamboo fiber also offers protection from the sun's UV rays, making it a great choice for summer garments.

Cashmere

Luxuriously soft, cashmere is a noble fiber. This "fiber of kings" can be up to eight times warmer than sheep's wool. Cashmere is spun from the fine, light wool or down hair taken from the undercoat of the Kashmir goat—an animal originally raised in central and south west Asia, particularly in Kashmir. The best cashmere is said to come from goats bred in both inner and outer Mongolia, where the extreme weather conditions encourage the growth of the finest underhair. It takes the underhair of two goats to make an average sweater.

The goat's fleece is combed by hand, rather than sheared, and the cashmere fiber is then carefully sorted into different colors and graded by eye, white being the most highly prized shade. Blends featuring cashmere are now widely offered, most commonly with merino wool, silk, or cotton.

Cotton

A natural vegetable fiber of great economic importance as a raw material for cloth. Its widespread use is largely due to the ease with which its fibers are spun into yarns, Cotton's strength, absorbency, and capacity to be washed and dyed also make it adaptable for a considerable variety of textile products.

Hemp

A perfect yarn for hand knitting. And a beautiful yarn, too: 100 percent natural, with a dry handle, subtle sheen, and natural drape. Cool in summer, repelling 90 percent of UV rays, and warm in winter, hemp is comfortable at all times. It is also a robust fiber that will last forever, getting softer each time it is washed and tumble dried.

Hemp is the world's leading renewable resource; it can grow in virtually any soil and climate. It is excellent for reclaiming otherwise unusable land, and as it is unpalatable to insects, it requires no pesticides. Importantly, nearly anything made from plastic, petroleum, wood, or cotton can be made from hemp. Knitting with hemp requires a little adjustment and slightly more time. Like linen, hemp has no natural elasticity, so once knitted, traditional methods of blocking and steaming enhance the appearance and softness of the finished fabric and create a truly timeless piece.

Donegal tweed

The landscape of County Donegal in the far northwest of Ireland is said to be the inspiration for this distinctive wool yarn. The rich colors reflect the tones and textures of the area, with its rocky mountains and heather-covered glens, wild seas, and hardy, independent people. For centuries, Donegal has produced tweed from local materials: wool fleeces provided by the sheep that thrive in hills and bogs of the region and natural plant dyes from indigenous species including blackberries, fuchsia, gorse, and moss.

Kid mohair

Mohair is a beautifully light and lustrous fiber taken from the angora goat (not to be confused with the angora rabbit). Despite its silky appearance, kid mohair is an extremely hardwearing fiber. The word "mohair" is a corruption of the ancient Arabic word "mukhyarr," which means "best of fleece." Native to Anchora in Turkey, but now successfully bred in the U.S. and Australia, the angora goat can be sheared twice a year to give a fleece of strong fibers. The best fleeces come from young animals aged between six months and four years. The absence of crimp means that the fibers do not felt. The best kid mohair is often finer than human hair.

Wool

Wool is a wonderful fiber: natural, biodegradable, and sustainable. For thousands of years, wool has provided the most effective, all-weather protection known to man. Wool has many inherent benefits that make it the ultimate fiber when it comes to comfort; it is breathable, it has natural stretch, and it regulates both temperature and moisture, dispersing water from the skin and helping to maintain a steady temperature. Wool of any type is a cosy fiber to envelope yourself in. It is an ideal choice for knitting either an outer garment or one to be worn close to the skin. A sweater made in natural wool is environmentally friendly; when a wool garment is disposed of, it decomposes back into the earth in a matter of years, as opposed to synthetic fibers that are extremely slow to degrade. Furthermore, wool is a completely renewable fiber source, as sheep produce new fleece each year.

Silk

Silk has long been considered the fiber of luxury and wealth, often known as the "queen of fibers." Despite its fineness, softness, and fluidity, silk is stronger than a steel rod. Silk is a continuous filament of protein substances secreted by the caterpillar, or silk worm of the bombyx mori moth, through a tiny hole in its lip; this is used to form the cocoon, which protects the larvae. The natural habitat for a silk worm is the mulberry tree, which is cultivated in large numbers for the breeding of the silk worm. Silk's absorbency gives infinite possibilities for dyeing, from deep, rich tones to subtle shades, providing a beautifully diverse palette.

Recommended yarns

The secret to getting the most out of a yarn is to experiment with it, trying out various needle sizes and seeing how it works in different stitch patterns. I have recommended a yarn type for each project, which is of good quality and specifically suited to the design of the garment. If you cannot find the particular yarn specified in the instructions, any other make of yarn that is of the same weight and type should serve as well; however to avoid disappointing results it is very important that you work a gauge swatch first that matches that given in the instructions, changing the needle size if necessary to achieve the correct gauge.

Substituting yarns

If you decide to use an alternative yarn, in order to find a specific shade or because you cannot obtain the yarn recommended, be sure to purchase a substitute yarn that is as close as possible to the original in thickness, weight, and texture so that it will be compatible with the knitting instructions. Buy only one ball to start with, so you can test the effect and the gauge. Calculate quantities required using the information about lengths (yardage or meterage) written on the yarn labels. The recommended knitting-needle size and knitting gauge on the yarn labels are extra guides to the yarn thickness. (See pages 138–139 for more yarn information.)

The instructions for each garment specifies the amount of yarn needed to complete the project in whichever size you choose. When purchasing yarn for a project it is sensible to buy a little more than is needed.

ABBREVIATIONS

All knitting patterns follow a basic structure and use the same standard abbreviations and terminology.

alt	alternate
approx	approximately
beg	begin, beginning
cm	centimeter(s)
cont	continue, continuing
DK	double knitting (a lightweight yarn)
dec	decrease, decreasing
foll	follows, following
g	gram(s)
garter st	garter stitch (k every row)
in	inch(es)
inc	increase, increasing
k	knit
LH	left hand
m	meter(s)
M1	make one stitch by picking up horizontal loop before next stitch and working into back of it
mm	millimeter(s)
oz	ounce(s)
p	purl
patt	pattern; *or* work in pattern
psso	pass slipped stitch over
rem	remains, remaining
rep	repeat, repeating
rev St st	reverse stockinette stitch (p all RS rows, k all WS rows)
RH	right hand
RS	right side
skp	slip 1, knit 1, pass slipped stitch over (one stitch decreased)
sl	slip
st(s)	stitch(es)
St st	stockinette stitch (k all RS rows, p all WS rows)
tbl	through back of loop(s)
tog	together
WS	wrong side
yd	yard(s)
yo	yarn over (yarn over right needle to make a new stitch)

[ ] * Repeat instructions between brackets, or after or between asterisks, as many times as instructed.

SIZING

With the exception of the hats and scarves in the accessories chapter, each garment is given in either three or five different sizes ranging from small to xxl. The smallest size is given first and appears outside the ( ) parentheses. The larger sizes are given inside the parentheses in ascending order. When working through the instructions, your size will be in the same position throughout the pattern. If only one number is given, it applies to all five of the sizes and where 0 appears no stitches or rows are worked for this size. You can always highlight the relevant instructions for your size within the pattern to avoid any confusion. Where instructions are given in [ ] brackets, work these instructions the number of times stated after the brackets.

The sizes of the garments are small, medium, large, xl, and xxl, and for each of these sizes a standard chest measurement is given. This size reflects the chest measurement of the wearer and not the finished dimensions of the garment, which are given as the "actual chest" measurements. Even though the chest measurement for a size, let's say small, is given consistently throughout the patterns as 36 inches, the "actual chest" measurement (knitted measurement) of different garments will vary depending on whether it is intended to be a slim-fit or a loose, more roomy design.

Alongside each knitting pattern is a detailed flat photograph of the finished garment with labels to indicate the final measurements for each size.

GENERAL GUIDELINES FOR YARN WEIGHTS

The Craft Yarn Council of America has instituted a number system for knitting and crochet yarn gauges and recommended needle and hook sizes. The information provided below is intended as a guideline, and as always, swatching is key to being sure a chosen yarn is a good match for the intended project. More information can be found at www.yarnstandards.com.

CYCA	🧶1	🧶2	🧶3	🧶4	🧶5
Yarn weight	SUPERFINE Lace, Fingering, Sock	FINE Sport	LIGHT DK, Light Worsted	MEDIUM Worsted, Aran	BULKY Chunky
Avg. Knitted Guage over 4" (10cm)	27–32 sts	23–26 sts	21–24 sts	16–20 sts	12–15 sts
Recommended Needle in US Size Range	1–3	3–5	5–7	7–9	9–11
Recommended Needle in Metric Size Range	2.25–3.25mm	3.25–3.75mm	3.75–4.5mm	4.5–5.5mm	5.5–8mm

* Guidelines Only: The above reflects the most commonly used gauges and needle or hook sies for specific yarn categories.

GARMENT CARE

When you invest so much time in creating a hand-knitted garment, great care should be taken in the laundering of these items. Depending on how a garment is worn, it may require fairly frequent washing. The yarn you use must be able to stand up to this, but this does not necessarily mean that all yarns must be machine-washable. Look at the labels: those on most commercial yarns have instructions for washing (or dry cleaning), drying and blocking. So, for a project knit in one yarn only, a quick look at the yarn label will tell you how to care for it. If you wish to work with several yarns in one piece of work, the aftercare requires a little more thought. If one label suggests dry cleaning, then be sure to dry clean the garment.

If in doubt about whether or not your knitwear is washable, make a little swatch of the yarns. Wash the swatch to see if the fabric is affected by being immersed in water or not, watching out for shrinkage and stretching. If you are satisfied with the results, go ahead and wash the knitted item by hand in lukewarm water. Never use hot water, as this may felt your fabric, and you will not be able to return it to its prewashed state. Take care, too, to keep the rinsing water the same temperature as the washing water. Wool in particular tends to react to major changes in temperature.

Always remember that natural fibers such as wool, cotton and silk are usually better washed by hand, and in pure soap, than in a machine.

Washing

When washing the finished knitting, handle it carefully. There should be enough water to cover the garment completely and the soap should be thoroughly dissolved before immersing it. If you need to wash any garment that has become badly soiled or stained, then use a commercial detergent. As a precaution, test-wash any readymade trims you use before you sew them onto the garment. Nothing is more infuriating then to spoil an entire garment because the trim colors run in the wash.

Rinsing

Squeeze out any excess water, never wring it out. Rinse thoroughly, until every trace of soap is removed, as any left in will mat the fibers and may irritate the skin. Use at least two changes of water or continue until the water is clear and contains no trace of soap bubbles.

Spinning

The garments can be rinsed on a short rinse and spun, as part of the normal washing machine program for delicate fabrics.

Drying

Squeeze the garment between towels or fold in a towel and gently spin. Do not hang wet knitting up to dry, as the weight of the water will stretch it out of shape. To dry, lay the knitting out flat on top of a towel, which will absorb some of the moisture. Ease the garment into shape. Keep the garment away from direct heat and leave flat until completely dry.

Blocking

When the garment is dry, ease it into shape. Check the yarn label before ironing your knitting as most fibers only require a little steam, and the iron should be applied gently. Alternatively, iron with a damp cloth between the garment and the iron.

Removing stains

Stains are a fact of life. The best solution with any stain is to remove the garment while the stain is still wet and soak it thoroughly in cold, never hot, water. Failing that, use a commercial stain remover.

basics

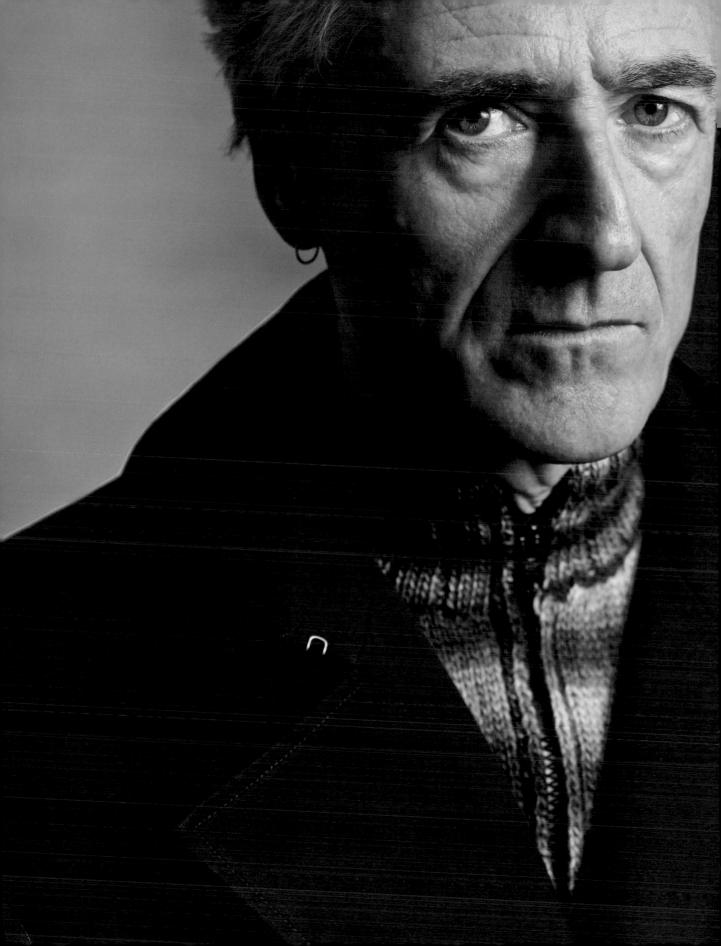

STRIPED FULL-ZIP CARDIGAN A basic

cardigan with a zipper closure is knit here in a self-striping yarn that gives a variegated color effect. This adds visual interest to the otherwise simple stockinette stitch. The finishing touches come in the form of the rib stitch detailing at the side seams, the patch pockets, and the neat "cyclist" collar.

sizes:

	s/m	m/l	xl/xxl	
to fit chest	36–38	38–40	42–44	inches
	92–97	97–102	107–112	cm
actual chest	44	46¾	50	inches
	112	119	127	cm
actual length	26	27	28¼	inches
	66	69	72	cm
sleeve length	18	19	19¾	inches
	46	48	50	cm

materials:

12 (13, 14) balls of Rowan Tapestry; 70% wool, 30% soybean fiber; color gray; 1¾ oz (50g) 131yd (120m), **3** light.

Sizes 3, 5, and 6 (3.25mm, 3.75mm, and 4mm) needles

26 (27, 28)in/65 (70, 70)cm open-ended zipper

gauge:

22 sts and 30 rows to 4" (10cm) square measured over St st using size 6 (4mm) needles. Always work a gauge swatch and change needle size if necessary.

tips and techniques:

As the front bands are integral, join new balls of yarn at side and armhole edges when working the two fronts. The side rib edge detail finishes after the armhole shaping.

Fully fashioned shaping

Decreasing on a knit row:
K3, k2tog, k to last 5 sts, k2tog tbl, k3.
Decreasing on a purl row:
P3, p2tog tbl, p to last 5 sts, p2tog, p3.
Increasing on a knit row:
K3, M1, k to last 3 sts, M1, k3.

to knit the back:

Using size 3 (3.25mm) needles, cast on 123 (133, 138) sts and work in rib as follows:
Row 1 (RS) [K3, p2] to last 3 sts, k3.
Row 2 [P3, k2] to last 3 sts, p3.
Rep last 2 rows until work measures 2¼" (6cm), ending with RS facing for next row and inc 2 (0, 3) sts evenly across center 93 (0, 108) sts of last row. **125 (133, 141) sts.**
Change to size 6 (4mm) needles and beg with a k row, work in St st with rib edges as follows:
Row 1 (RS) [K3, p2] 3 times, k to last 15 sts, [p2, k3] 3 times.
Row 2 [P3, k2] 3 times, p to last 15 sts, [k2, p3] 3 times.
Rep last 2 rows until back measures 17¼ (17½, 18)" (44 [45, 46]cm), ending with RS facing for next row.

shape armholes

Bind off 6 sts at beg of next 2 rows. **113 (121, 129) sts.**
Dec 1 st (see note on fully fashioned shaping above) at each end of next 5 rows, then on foll 2 alt rows. **99 (107, 115) sts.**
Work even in St st only until armhole measures 8¾ (9½, 10¼)" (22 [24, 26]cm), ending with RS facing for next row.

shape shoulder and back neck

Bind off 10 (11, 12) sts at beg of next 2 rows. **79 (85, 91) sts.**
Next row Bind off 10 (11, 12) sts, work until there are 14 (15, 16) sts on RH needle, turn and work on these

sts only for first side of neck.
Bind off 4 sts at beg of next row.
Bind off rem 10 (11, 12) sts.
With RS of work facing, slip center 31 (33, 35) sts onto holder, rejoin yarn to rem sts and work to end of row.
Complete to match first side, reversing shaping.

to knit the left front:

Using size 3 (3.25mm) needles, cast on 62 (67, 72) sts and work in rib as follows:
Row 1 (RS) [K3, p2] to last 2 sts, k2.
Row 2 P2, [k2, p3] to end of row.
Rep last 2 rows until front measures 2$\frac{1}{4}$" (6cm) from cast-on edge, ending with RS facing for next row and inc 1 (0, dec 1) st in center of last row. **63 (67, 71) sts.**
Change to size 6 (4mm) needles and beg with a k row, work in St st with rib edges as follows:
Row 1 (RS) [K3, p2] 3 times, k to last 4 sts, p2, k2.
Row 2 P2, k2, p to last 15 sts, [k2, p3] 3 times.
Rep last 2 rows until front measures 17$\frac{1}{4}$ (17$\frac{1}{2}$, 18)" (44 [45, 46]cm), ending with RS facing for next row.

shape armholes
Next row (RS) Bind off 6 sts, k to last 4 sts, p2, k2.
Next row P2, k2, p to end of row.
Keeping 4 sts at center front in rib as set, dec 1 st at armhole edge on next 5 rows, then on foll 2 RS rows. **50 (54, 58) sts.**
Work even until armhole measures 6$\frac{3}{4}$ (7$\frac{1}{2}$, 8$\frac{1}{4}$)" (17 [19, 21]cm), ending with RS facing for next row.
Next row K to last 4 sts, turn and leave these
4 rib sts on a holder.

shape neck
Bind off 8 sts at beg of next row.
Dec 1 st (see note on fully fashioned shaping, page 22) at neck edge on next 5 (6, 7) rows, then on foll 3 RS rows. **30 (33, 36) sts.**
Work even until armhole measures 8$\frac{3}{4}$ (9$\frac{1}{2}$, 10$\frac{1}{4}$)" (22 [24, 26]cm), ending with RS facing for next row.
Bind off 10 (11, 12) sts at beg of

next row and foll RS row.
Work 1 row.
Bind off rem 10 (11, 12) sts.

to knit the right front:

Using size 3 (3.25mm) needles, cast on 62 (67, 72) sts and work in rib as follows:
Row 1 (RS) K2, [p2, k3] to end of row.
Row 2 [P3, k2] to last 2 sts, p2.
Rep last 2 rows until front measures 2$\frac{1}{4}$" (6cm) from cast-on edge, ending with RS facing for next row and inc 1 (0, dec 1) st in center of last row. **63 (67, 71) sts.**
Change to size 6 (4mm) needles and beg with a k row, work in St st with rib edges as follows:
Row 1 (RS) K2, p2, k to last 15 sts, [p2, k3] 3 times.
Row 2 [P3, k2] 3 times, p to last 4 sts, k2, p2.
Rep last 2 rows until front measures 17$\frac{1}{4}$ (17$\frac{1}{2}$, 18)" (44 [45, 46]cm), ending with WS facing for next row.

s/m 18" / 46cm
m/l 19" / 48cm
xl/xxl 19$\frac{3}{4}$" / 50cm

s/m 44" / 112cm
m/l 46$\frac{3}{4}$" / 119cm
xl/xxl 50" / 127cm

s/m 26" / 66cm
m/l 27" / 69cm
xl/xxl 28$\frac{1}{4}$" / 72cm

shape armhole

Next row (WS) Bind off 6 sts, p to last 4 sts, k2, p2.
Keeping 4 sts at center front in rib as set, work in St st
and dec 1 st at armhole edge of next 5 rows, then on
foll 2 RS rows. **50 (54, 58) sts.**
Work even until armhole measures 6¾ (7½, 8¼)"
(17 [19, 21]cm), ending with WS facing for next row.
Next row Work to last 4 sts, turn and leave these 4 rib
sts on a holder.

shape neck

Bind off 8 sts at beg of next row.
Dec 1 st (see note on fully fashioned shaping, page 22)
at neck edge on next 5 (6, 7) rows, then on foll 3 RS
rows.
30 (33, 36) sts.
Work even until armhole measures 8¾ (9½, 10¼)in/
22 (24, 26)cm, ending with WS facing for next row.
Bind off 10 (11, 12) sts at beg of next row and foll
WS row.
Work 1 row.
Bind off rem 10 (11, 12) sts.

to knit the sleeves:

Using size 3 (3.25mm) needles, cast on 47 (52, 57) sts.
Row 1 (RS) K2, [p2, k3] to end of row.
Row 2 [P3, k2] to last 2 sts, p2.
These 2 rows form rib and are repeated.
Work 3¼in/8cm in rib, ending with RS facing for next
row and inc 3 sts evenly across last row. **50 (55, 60) sts.**
Change to size 6 (4mm) needles and beg with a k row,
work in St st, inc 1 st (see note on fully fashioned
shaping, page 22) at each end of 3rd and every foll 6th
row until there are 88 (93, 98) sts.
Work even until sleeve measures 18 (19, 19¾)in/
46 (48, 50)cm from cast-on edge, ending with RS
facing for next row.

shape top of sleeve

Bind off 6 sts at beg of next 2 rows. **76 (81, 86) sts.**
Dec 1 st at each end of next 9 rows. **58 (63, 68) sts.**
Dec 1 st at each end of 11 (12, 13) foll RS rows, then
on foll 7 rows. **22 (25, 28) sts.**
Bind off 4 sts at beg of next 2 rows.
Bind off rem 14 (17, 20) sts.

to knit the collar:

Sew shoulder seams.
With RS facing and size 5 (3.75mm) needles, pick up
and rib 4 sts as set from right front holder, pick up and
k 29 (31, 32) sts up right front neck, 4 sts down right
back neck, k across 31 (33, 35) sts from back neck
holder, pick up and k 4 (5, 4) sts up left back neck and
29 (31, 32) sts down left front neck, then rib the 4 sts
from left front holder. **106 (111, 116) sts.**
Work in rib as follows:
Row 1 (WS) P2, [k2, p3] to last 4 sts, k2, p2.
Row 2 K2, p2, [k3, p2] to last 2 sts, k2.
Rep last 2 rows until collar measures 2¼in/6cm.
Change to size 3 (3.25mm) needles and work
2¼in/6cm more, ending with RS facing for next row.
Bind off loosely using size 5 (3.75mm) needle.

to knit the pockets:

(Make 2)
Using size 6 (4mm) needles, cast on 33 sts and beg
with a k row, work in St st until work measures
4¾ (4¾, 5)in/12 (12, 13)cm from cast-on edge, ending
with RS facing for next row.
Next row K3, [p2, k3] to end of row.
Next row P3, [k2, p3] to end of row.
Rep last 2 rows until work measures 6 (6, 6¼)in/
15 (15, 16)cm from cast-on edge, ending with RS facing
for next row.
Bind off.

to finish:

Weave in any yarn ends.
Lay work out flat and gently steam each piece.
Sew sleeves into armholes, easing to fit.
Sew side and sleeve seams from armhole to cuff edge
and hem, using mattress stitch.
Hand sew zipper in place behind ribbed front edges,
working from halfway up collar down to lower edge.
Fold collar to inside and slipstitch loosely in position
around neck edge and sew row ends to zipper tape.
Place pocket on each front, approx 2in/5cm away from
zipper and approx 9¾ (10¾, 11½)in/25 (27, 29)cm
down from top of shoulder, then sew in position.

WEEK DAY SWEATER

A simple V-neck sweater worked in a merino wool and cashmere blend offers real comfort—and the bulky-weight yarn makes this a relatively quick knit. The sweater is worked in stockinette stitch, with a fine contrasting color edging that adds a "lift" to the neck and sleeve trim.

sizes:

	s	m	l	xl	xxl	
to fit chest	36	38	40	42	44	inches
	92	97	102	107	112	cm
actual chest	42	43$\frac{1}{4}$	44$\frac{1}{2}$	45$\frac{3}{4}$	46$\frac{3}{4}$	inches
	107	110	113	116	119	cm
actual length	24$\frac{3}{4}$	25$\frac{1}{2}$	26$\frac{1}{4}$	27	28	inches
	63	65	67	69	71	cm
sleeve length	18	19	19$\frac{3}{4}$	19$\frac{3}{4}$	20$\frac{1}{2}$	inches
	46	48	50	50	52	cm

materials:

15 (16, 17, 18, 18) balls of Debbie Bliss Cashmerino Chunky; 55% merino wool, 33% microfiber, 12% cashmere; color duck egg blue (A) and chocolate brown (B); 1$\frac{3}{4}$ oz (50g) 70yd (65m), **⑤** bulky in A and 1 ball in B.

Sizes 10 and 10$\frac{1}{2}$ (6.5mm and 7mm) needles

Tapestry needle

gauge:

14 sts and 22 rows to 4" (10cm) square measured over St st using size 10$\frac{1}{2}$ (7mm) needles. Always work a gauge swatch and change needle size if necessary.

tips and techniques:

Fully fashioned shaping
Decreasing on a knit row:
K3, k2tog, k to last 5 sts, k2tog tbl, k3.
Decreasing on a purl row:
P3, p2tog tbl, p to last 5 sts, p2tog, p3.
Increasing on a knit row:
K3, M1, k to last 3 sts, M1, k3.

to knit the back:

Using size 10 (6.5mm) and A, cast on 77 (77, 77, 82, 82) sts and work in rib as follows:

Row 1 (RS) [K3, p2] to last 2 sts, k2.

Row 2 P2, [k2, p3] to end of row.

Rep last 2 rows until work measures 3¼" (8cm), ending with RS facing for next row and inc 0 (2, 4, 1, 3) sts evenly across last row. **77 (79, 81, 83, 85) sts.**

Change to size 10½ (7mm) needles and beg with a k row, work in St st until back measures 16 (16½, 16¾, 17¼, 17½)" (41 [42, 43, 44, 45])cm from cast-on edge, ending with RS facing for next row.

shape armholes

Bind off 4 sts at beg of next 2 rows. **69 (71, 73, 75, 77) sts.**

Dec 1 st (see note on fully fashioned shaping, page 28) at each end of next row and foll 2 RS rows. **63 (65, 67, 69, 71) sts. ****

Work even until armhole measures 8¾ (9, 9½, 9¾, 10½)" (22 [23, 24, 25, 26])cm, ending with RS facing for next row.

shape shoulders and back neck

Next row Bind off 8 (9, 9, 10, 10) sts, k until there are 13 sts on RH needle, turn and work on these sts only for first side of neck.

Bind off 4 sts at beg of next row.

Bind off rem 9 sts.

With RS facing, slip center 21 (21, 23, 23, 25) sts onto a holder, rejoin yarn to rem sts and work to end of row. Complete to match first side, reversing shaping.

to knit the front:

Work as given for Back to **.

Work even until front measures 18 (18½, 18¾, 19¼, 19½)" (46 [47, 48, 49, 50])cm, ending with RS facing for next row.

divide for neck

Next row K31 (32, 33, 34, 35) sts, turn and leave rem sts on a holder.

Next row P.

Next row K to last 4 sts, k2tog tbl, k2.

Next row P.

Rep last 2 rows until 17 (18, 18, 19, 19) sts rem.

Work even until armhole measures 8¾ (9, 9½, 9¾,

10½)" (22 [23, 24, 25, 26])cm, ending with RS facing for next row.

shape shoulder

Bind off 8 (9, 9, 10, 10) sts at beg of next row.

Work 1 row.

Bind off rem 9 sts.

With RS facing, place center front st on a holder, rejoin yarn to rem 31 (32, 33, 34, 35) sts and k to end of row.

Work 1 row.

Next row K2, k2tog, k to end of row.

Next row P.

Rep last 2 rows until 17 (18, 18, 19, 19) sts rem.

Work even until armhole measures 8¾ (9, 9½, 9¾, 10½)" (22 [23, 24, 25, 26])cm, ending with WS facing for next row.

shape shoulder

Bind off 8 (9, 9, 10, 10) sts at beg of next row.

Work 1 row.

Bind off rem 9 sts.

to knit the sleeves:

Using size 10 (6.5mm) needles and B, cast on 32 (32, 37, 37, 37) sts,

Change to A and work 3¼" (8cm) in rib as given for Back, ending with RS facing for next row and inc 1 (3, 0, 2, 2) sts evenly across last row. **33 (35, 37, 39, 39) sts.**

Change to size 10½ (7mm) needles and beg with a k row, work in St st, inc 1 st (see note on fully fashioned shaping, page 28) at each end of 3rd and every foll 8th row until there are 51 (53, 57, 59, 61) sts.

Work even until sleeve measures 18 (19, 19¾, 19¾, 20½)" (46 [48, 50, 50, 52])cm from cast-on edge, ending with RS facing for next row.

shape top of sleeve

Bind off 4 sts at beg of next 2 rows. **43 (45, 49, 51, 53) sts.**

Dec 1 st (see note on fully fashioned shaping, page 28) at each end of next row and every foll RS row until 23 (25, 29, 31, 33) sts rem.

Dec 1 st at each end of next 5 (6, 7, 8, 9) rows. **13 (13, 15, 15, 15) sts.**

Bind off 3 sts at beg of next 2 rows.

Bind off rem 7 (7, 9, 9, 9) sts.

s 42" / 107cm
m 43¼" / 110cm
l 44½" / 113cm
xl 45¾" / 116cm
xxl 46¾" / 119cm

s 18" / 46cm
m 19" / 48cm
l 19¾" / 50cm
xl 19¾" / 50cm
xxl 20½" / 52cm

s 24¾" / 63cm
m 25½" / 65cm
l 26¼" / 67cm
xl 27" / 69cm
xxl 28" / 71cm

to knit the neckband:

Sew right shoulder seam.

With RS facing, size 10 (6.5mm) needles, and A, pick up and k 30 (30, 33, 33, 36) sts down left front neck, k 1 st from center front holder and mark with a colored thread, pick up and k 30 (30, 33, 33, 36) sts up right front neck, then 30 sts around back neck, including sts on back neck holder. 91 (91, 97, 97, 103) sts.

Work in rib as follows:

Row 1 (WS) [P2, k1] to marked stitch, p1, [k1, p2] to end of row.

Row 2 (RS) Rib as set to 2 sts before marked stitch, p2tog, k1, p2tog tbl, rib as set to end.

Row 3 Rib as set.

Rep rows 2 and 3 until neckband measures 1½" (3.5cm), ending with WS facing for next row.
Change to B and work 1 row in rib as set.
Bind off in rib.

to finish:

Weave in any yarn ends.
Lay work out flat and gently steam each piece.
Sew left shoulder and neckband seam.
Sew sleeves into armholes, easing to fit.
Sew side and sleeve seams, from armhole to cuff edge and hem, using mattress stitch.

1950s STYLE CARDIGAN
A retro-inspired zipper cardigan with a garter stitch collar and patch pockets, made in lofty but lightweight wool with oversized stitches. It is worked in stockinette stitch with a contrasting rib-stitch back. This garment knits up fast and is a great basic.

sizes:

	s	m	l	xl	xxl	
to fit chest	36	38	40	42	44	inches
	92	97	102	107	112	cm
actual chest	44	46	48	50	52	inches
	112	117	122	127	132	cm
actual length	26	26¾	27½	28¼	29	inches
	66	68	70	72	74	cm
sleeve length	17¼	17¼	18	18	19	inches
	44	44	46	46	48	cm

materials:

10 (11, 11, 12, 12) balls of Rowan Big Wool; 100% merino wool; color mulberry; 3½oz (100g) 126yd (115m), **5** bulky.

Sizes 15 and 17 (10mm and 12mm) needles

22 (24, 24, 26, 26)" (55 [60, 60, 65, 65])cm heavyweight open-ended zipper

Tapestry needle

gauge:

8 sts and 10–12 rows to 4" (10cm) square measured over St st using size 17 (12mm) needles. Always work a gauge swatch and change needle size if necessary.

tips and techniques:

Fully fashioned shaping
Decreasing on a knit row:
K3, k2tog, k to last 5 sts, k2tog tbl, k3.
Decreasing on a purl row:
P3, p2tog tbl, p to last 5 sts, p2tog, p3.
Increasing on a knit row:
K3, M1, k to last 3 sts, M1, k3.

to knit the back:

Using size 15 (10mm) needles, cast on 46 (48, 50, 52, 54) sts and work in rib as follows:
Row 1 (RS) P3 (1, 2, 3, 1), k1, [p2, k1] to last 3 (1, 2, 3, 1), p3 (1, 2, 3, 1).
Row 2 K3 (1, 2, 3, 1), p1, [k2, p1] to last 3 (1, 2, 3, 1), k3 (1, 2, 3, 1).
Rep last 2 rows until work measures 3¼" (8cm), ending with RS facing for next row.
Change to size 17 (12mm) needles and cont in rib as set until work measures 16½ (17, 17¼, 17¾, 18)" (42 [43, 44, 45, 46])cm from cast-on edge, ending with RS facing for next row.

shape armholes
Bind off 3 sts at beg next 2 rows. 40 (42, 44, 46, 48) sts.
Next row (RS) P2, k2tog, rib as set to last 4 sts, k2tog, p2.
Next row K2, p2tog, rib as set to last 4 sts, p2tog, k2.
Next row P2, k2tog, rib as set to last 4 sts, k2tog, p2.
34 (36, 38, 40, 42) sts.
Work even in rib as set until armhole measures 9½ (9¾, 10¼, 10½, 11)" (24 [25, 26, 27, 28])cm, ending with RS facing for next row.

shape shoulders and back neck
Next row Bind off 5 (5, 6, 6, 6) sts, rib until there are 8 (8, 9, 9, 9) sts on RH needle, turn and work on these sts only for first side of neck.

s 44" / 112cm
m 46" / 117cm
l 48" / 122cm
xl 50" / 127cm
xxl 52" / 132cm

s 17¼" / 44cm
m 17¼" / 44cm
l 18" / 46cm
xl 18" / 46cm
xxl 19" / 48cm

s 26" / 66cm
m 26¾" / 68cm
l 27½" / 70cm
xl 28¼" / 72cm
xxl 29" / 74cm

Bind off 3 sts at beg of next row.

Bind off rem 5 (5, 5, 6, 7) sts.

With RS facing, rejoin yarn to rem sts, bind off center 8 (10, 10, 10, 10) sts and rib to end of row.

Complete to match first side, reversing shaping.

to knit the left front:

Using size 15 (10mm) needles, cast on 24 (25, 26, 27, 28) sts and work in rib with garter stitch edge as follows:

Row 1 (RS) K0 (1, 2, 0, 1), p1, [k2, p1] to last 2 sts, k2.

Row 2 K2, [k1, p2] to last 1 (2, 3, 1, 2) sts, k1, p0 (1, 2, 0, 1, 2).

Rep last 2 rows until work measures 3¼" (8cm), ending with RS facing for next row.

Change to size 17 (12mm) needles and beg with a k row, work in St st with garter stitch front edge as follows:

Row 1 (RS) K.

Row 2 K2, p to end of row.

Rep last 2 rows until work measures 16½ (17, 17¼, 17¾, 18)" (42 [43, 44, 45, 46])cm from cast-on edge, ending with RS facing for next row.

shape armhole

Bind off 3 sts at beg of next row. **21 (22, 23, 24, 25) sts.** Work 1 row.

Dec 1 st at armhole edge on next 3 rows. **18 (19, 20, 21, 22) sts.**

Work even until front measures 22¾ (23½, 24½, 25½, 26)" (58 [60, 62, 65, 66])cm, ending with WS facing for next row.

shape neck

Bind off 5 sts at beg of next row. **13 (14, 15, 16, 17) sts.** Dec 1 st (see note for fully fashioned shaping, page 32) at neck edge on next 3 (4, 4, 4, 4) rows. **10 (10, 11, 12, 13) sts.**

Work even until armhole measures 9½ (9¾, 10¼, 10½, 11)" (24 [25, 26, 27, 28])cm, ending with RS facing for next row.

shape shoulder

Bind off 5 (5, 6, 6, 6) sts at beg of next row.

Work 1 row. Bind off rem 5 (5, 5, 6, 7) sts.

to knit the right front:

Using size 15 (10mm) needles, cast on 24 (25, 26, 27, 28) sts and work in rib with garter stitch edge as follows:

Row 1 (RS) [K2, p1] to last 0 (1, 2, 0, 1, 2) sts, k0 (1, 2, 0, 1).

Row 2 P0 (1, 2, 0, 1, 2), k1, [p2, k1] to last 2 sts, k2.

Rep last 2 rows until work measures 3¼" (8cm), ending with RS facing for next row.

Change to size 17 (12mm) needles and beg with a k row, work in St st with garter stitch front edge as follows:

Row 1 (RS) K.

Row 2 P to last 2 sts, k2.

Rep last 2 rows until work measures 16½ (17, 17¼, 17¾, 18)" (42 [43, 44, 45, 46])cm from cast-on edge, ending with WS facing for next row.

shape armhole

Bind off 3 sts at beg of next row. **21 (22, 23, 24, 25) sts.**

Dec 1 st (see note on fully fashioned shaping, page 32) at armhole edge on next 3 rows. **18 (19, 20, 21, 22) sts.**

Work even until front measures 22¾ (23½, 24½, 25½, 26)" (58 [60, 62, 65, 66])cm, ending with RS facing for next row.

shape neck

Bind off 5 sts at beg of next row. **13 (14, 15, 16, 17) sts.**

Dec 1 st at neck edge on next 3 (4, 4, 4, 4) rows. **10 (10, 11, 12, 13) sts.**

Work even until armhole measures 9½ (9¾, 10¼, 10½, 11)" (24 [25, 26, 27, 28])cm, ending with WS facing for next row.

shape shoulder

Bind off 5 (5, 6, 6, 6) sts at beg of next row.

Work 1 row. Bind off rem 5 (5, 5, 6, 7) sts.

to knit the sleeves:

Using size 15 (10mm) needles, cast on 29 (29, 32, 32, 35) sts and work in rib as follows:

Row 1 (RS) [K2, p1] to last 2 sts, k2.

Row 2 [P2, k1] to last 2 sts, p2.

Rep last 2 rows until work measures 3¼" (8cm), ending with RS facing for next row.

Change to size 17 (12mm) and beg with a k row, work in St st, inc 1 st (see note on fully fashioned shaping, page 32) at each end of 5th and every foll 6th row until there are 41 (41, 44, 44, 47) sts.

Work even until sleeve measures 17¼ (17¼, 18, 18, 19)" (44 [44, 46, 46, 48])cm from cast-on edge, ending with RS facing for next row.

shape top of sleeve

Bind off 3 sts at beg of next 2 rows. **35 (35, 38, 38, 41) sts.**

Dec 1 st at each end of next row and 3 foll RS rows. Work 1 row. Bind off rem 27 (27, 30, 30, 33) sts.

to knit the collar:

Using size 15 (10mm) needles, cast on 4 sts and beg with a RS row (place marker at start of this row so that you know which is the RS of work), work in garter st (k every row) as follows:

Inc 1 st each end of next row and foll 2 RS rows. **10 sts.** Work 1 row. (RS of work facing for next row.)

Inc 1 st at beg of next row and foll 2 RS rows. **16 sts.** Work even in garter st for 31 (35, 35, 35, 35) rows, ending with RS facing for next row.

Dec 1 st at beg of next row and foll 2 RS rows. **10 sts.** Work 1 row.

Dec 1 st at each end of next row and foll 2 RS rows. Bind off rem 4 sts.

to knit the pockets:

Using size 17 (12mm) needles, cast on 10 (12, 12, 12, 12) sts and beg with a k row, work 4¾" (12cm) in St st, ending with WS facing for next row.

Change to size 15 (10mm) needles and k 4 rows, so ending with WS facing for next row. Bind off knitwise.

to finish:

Weave in any yarn ends.

Lay work out flat and gently steam each piece.

Sew both shoulder seams.

Sew sleeves into armholes, easing to fit.

Sew side and sleeve seams from armhole to cuff edge and hem, using with mattress stitch.

With top of zipper aligned with start of neck shaping, hand sew zipper to fronts, behind garter st edge.

Sew on pockets with invisible stitch.

With center of collar edge to center of back neck, stitch collar in place around neck edge, easing to fit.

Attach a short length of yarn to zipper pull.

HALF-ZIP SWEATER

A great casual piece for weekend wear—a simple long-sleeved sweater with a collar, half zipper, and breast pocket detail. Lengthen the life of this robust sweater with the optional knitted elbow patches, which will not wear out.

sizes:

	s	m	l	xl	xxl	
to fit chest	36	38	40	42	44	inches
	92	97	102	107	112	cm
actual chest	42$\frac{1}{2}$	44$\frac{1}{2}$	46	48	49$\frac{1}{2}$	inches
	108	113	117	122	126	cm
actual length	27$\frac{1}{4}$	27$\frac{1}{2}$	28	28$\frac{1}{4}$	28$\frac{3}{4}$	inches
	69	70	71	72	73	cm
sleeve length	19	19$\frac{1}{4}$	19$\frac{3}{4}$	20$\frac{1}{2}$	20$\frac{1}{2}$	inches
	48	49	50	52	52	cm

materials:

19 (20, 21, 22, 23) balls of Rowan Classic Cashsoft Aran; 57% extra fine merino wool, 33% microfiber, 10% cashmere; color mid blue; 1$\frac{3}{4}$ oz (50g) 95yd (87m); (4) medium.

Sizes 7 and 8 (4.5mm and 5mm) needles

Size 7 (4.5mm) circular needle

10" (25cm) zipper

Approx 28" (70cm) of 1" (2.5cm) wide cotton tape (optional)

gauge:

18 sts and 24 rows to 4" (10cm) square measured over St st using size 8 (5mm) needles. Always work a gauge swatch and change needle size if necessary.

tips and techniques:

Fully fashioned shaping
Decreasing on a knit row:
K3, k2tog, k to last 5 sts, k2tog tbl, k3.
Decreasing on a purl row:
P3, p2tog tbl, p to last 5 sts, p2tog, p3.
Increasing on a knit row:
K3, M1, k to last 3 sts, M1, k3.

to knit the back:

Using size 7 (4.5mm) needles, cast on 100 (104, 108, 112, 116) sts and work 1 row in k1, p1 rib.
Change to size 8 (5mm) needles and beg with a k row, work in St st until back measures 18$\frac{1}{2}$" (47cm) from cast-on edge, ending with RS facing for next row.

shape armholes

Bind off 4 sts at beg of next 2 rows. 92 (96, 100, 104, 108) sts.

Dec 1 st (see note on fully fashioned shaping above) at each end of next 3 rows and foll 2 RS rows. 82 (86, 90, 94, 98) sts rem. ***

Work even until armhole measures 8$\frac{3}{4}$ (9, 9$\frac{1}{2}$, 9$\frac{3}{4}$, 10$\frac{1}{4}$)" (22 [23, 24, 25, 26])cm, ending with RS facing for next row.

shape shoulders and back neck

Bind off 8 (9, 9, 10, 10) sts at beg of next 2 rows. 66 (68, 72, 74, 78) sts.

Next row Bind off 8 (9, 9, 10, 10) sts, k until there are 12 (12, 13, 13, 14) sts on RH needle, turn and work on these sts only for first side of neck.
Bind off 4 sts at beg of next row.
Cast of rem 8 (8, 9, 9, 10) sts.
With RS facing, slip center 26 (26, 28, 28, 30) sts onto holder, rejoin yarn and k to end of row.
Complete to match first side, reversing shaping.

s 42½" / 108cm
m 44½" / 113cm
l 46" / 117cm
xl 48" / 122cm
xxl 49½" / 126cm

s 19" / 48cm
m 19¼" / 49cm
l 19¾" / 50cm
xl 20½" / 52cm
xxl 20½" / 52cm

s 27¼" / 69cm
m 27½" / 70cm
l 28" / 71cm
xl 28¼" / 72cm
xxl 28¾" / 73cm

to knit the front:

Work as given for Back to ***.

P 1 row.

divide for neck opening

Next row (RS) K39 (41, 43, 45, 47), p1, k1, turn and leave rem 41 (43, 45, 47, 49) sts on a holder.

Work each side separately.

Next row P1, k1, p to end of row.

Next row K to last 2 sts, p1, k1.

Next row P1, k1, p to end of row.

Rep last 2 rows until front measures 26¼" (67cm) from cast-on edge, ending with RS facing for next row.

shape neck

Next row K39 (41, 43, 45, 47) sts, turn and leave 2 rib sts on a holder.

Bind off 7 (7, 8, 8, 9) sts at beg of next row. **32 (34, 35, 37, 38) sts.**

Dec 1 st (see note on fully fashioned shaping, page 38) at neck edge on next 7 rows, then on foll RS row, **and at the same time** when armhole measures 8¾ (9, 9½, 9¾, 10¼)" (22 [23, 24, 25, 26])cm and ending with RS

facing for next row, shape shoulder as follows:

shape shoulder

Bind off 8 (9, 9, 10, 10) sts at beg of next row and foll RS row.

Work 1 row.

Bind off rem 8 (8, 9, 9, 10) sts.

With RS facing, rejoin yarn to 41 (43, 45, 47, 49) sts on holder and work as follows:

Next row K1, p1, k to end of row.

Next row P to last 2 sts, k1, p1.

Complete to match first side, reversing shaping.

to knit the sleeves:

Using size 7 (4.5mm) needles, cast on 44 (44, 44, 47, 47) sts and work in rib as follows:

Row 1 (RS) [K2, p1] to last 2 sts, k2.

Row 2 [P2, k1] to last 2 sts, p2.

Rep last 2 rows until work measures 3¼" (8cm), ending with RS facing for next row and inc 0 (0, 0, 1, 1) st on last row. **44 (44, 44, 48, 48) sts.**

Change to size 8 (5mm) needles and beg with a k row, work in St st, inc 1 st (see note on fully fashioned shaping, page 38) at each end of 5th and every foll 6th row until there are 60 (60, 62, 64, 66) sts, then on 5 foll 8th rows. **70 (70, 72, 74, 76) sts.**

Work even until sleeve measures 19 (19$\frac{1}{4}$, 19$\frac{3}{4}$, 20$\frac{1}{2}$, 20$\frac{1}{2}$)" (48 [49, 50, 52, 52])cm from cast-on edge, ending with RS facing for next row.

shape top of sleeve

Bind off 4 sts at beg of next 2 rows. **62 (62, 64, 66, 68) sts.**

Dec 1 st at each end of next 3 rows. **56 (56, 58, 60, 62) sts.**

Now dec 1 st at each end of next 2 (2, 2, 3, 3) RS rows, then 2 foll 4th rows. **48 (48, 50, 50, 52) sts.**

Work 1 row.

Dec 1 st at each end of next row and foll 4 (4, 4, 3, 3) RS rows. **38 (38, 40, 42, 44) sts.**

Now dec 1 st at each end of next 9 rows. **20 (20, 22, 24, 26) sts.**

Bind off 4 sts at beg of next 2 rows.

Bind off rem 12 (12, 14, 16, 18) sts.

to knit the collar:

Weave in any yarn ends.

Lay work out flat and gently steam each piece.

Graft both shoulder seams.

With RS facing and size 7 (4.5mm) circular needle, rib 2 sts as set from right front holder, pick up and k 24 (24, 25, 25, 25) sts up right front neck, and 6 sts down right back neck, then k 26 (26, 28, 28, 30) sts from back neck holder, pick up and k 6 sts up left back neck, and 24 (24, 24, 24, 25) sts down left neck, then rib 2 sts as set from left front holder. **90 (90, 93, 93, 96) sts.**

Next row (WS) P1, k1, [p2, k1] to last 4 sts, p2, k1, p1.

Next row K1, p1, [k2, p1] to last 4 sts, k2, p1, k1.

Rep last 2 rows until collar measures 3$\frac{1}{2}$" (9cm), ending with RS facing for next row. Bind off in rib.

to knit the pocket:

(Make 1)

Using size 7 (4.5mm) needles, cast on 24 (24, 24, 26, 26) sts and work 2 rows in k1, p1 rib.

Change to size 8 (5mm) needles and beg with a k row, work in St st until pocket measures 4$\frac{3}{4}$ (4$\frac{3}{4}$, 4$\frac{3}{4}$, 5, 5)" (12 [12, 12, 13, 13])cm from cast-on edge, ending with RS facing for next row.

Dec 1 st (see note on fully fashioned shaping, page 38) at each end of next row and foll 3 RS rows. **16 (16, 16, 18, 18) sts.**

P 1 row.

Bind off.

to make the elbow patches:

(Make 2—optional)

Using size 8 (5mm) needles, cast on 18 sts and beg with a k row, work in St st, inc 1 st (see note on fully fashioned shaping, page 38) at each end of 3rd row and foll 2 RS rows. **24 sts.**

Work even until patch measures 7$\frac{1}{2}$" (19cm) from cast-on edge, ending with RS facing for next row.

Dec 1 st (see note on fully fashioned shaping, page 38) at each end of next row and foll 2 RS rows.

Work even for 3 rows.

Bind off.

to finish:

Weave in any yarn ends.

Lay work out flat and gently steam each piece.

Sew sleeves into armholes, easing to fit.

Sew side and sleeve seams, using mattress stitch.

Sew on pocket approx 7$\frac{3}{4}$" (20cm) down from shoulder, and elbow patches to sleeves.

Hand sew zipper in place behind ribbed front opening edges to top of collar edge.

optional trim:

Cut a strip of cotton tape to cover each side of zipper on the inside of the sweater and sew in place.

To give a casual detail, cut a strip of 1" wide cotton tape approx 5$\frac{1}{2}$ (5$\frac{1}{2}$, 5$\frac{1}{2}$, 6, 6)" (14 [14, 14, 15, 15])cm long, then fold lengthwise over pocket top and sew in position, tucking raw ends under to neaten.

CASUAL CARDIGAN

This cardigan design is a quintessential basic—long-sleeved with a V-neck and double ribbing. The buttonhole and button bands are worked integrally while knitting to avoid extra stretching and sewing and for a much neater finish. It is worked in hemp: an ancient, natural and sustainable fiber that is gaining renewed popularity due to its unique properties. The buttons are natural horn, also from sustainable sources, and enhance the subtle tones of the yarn.

sizes:

	s	m	l	xl	xxl	
to fit chest	36	38	40	42	44	inches
	92	97	102	107	112	cm
actual chest	42$\frac{1}{2}$	44$\frac{3}{4}$	46$\frac{3}{4}$	49$\frac{1}{4}$	51$\frac{1}{4}$	inches
	108	114	119	125	130	cm
actual length	25$\frac{3}{4}$	26$\frac{1}{4}$	27	28	28$\frac{3}{4}$	inches
	65	67	69	71	73	cm
sleeve length	18$\frac{1}{2}$	19	19	19$\frac{1}{4}$	19$\frac{1}{4}$	inches
	47	48	48	49	49	cm

materials:

9 (9, 10, 10, 11) skeins of Lanaknits Hemp for Knitting Allhemp6; 100% hemp; color ecru; 3$\frac{1}{2}$oz (100g) 165yd (150m); **3** light.

Sizes 3 and 5 (3.25mm and 3.75mm) needles

5 natural horn buttons, 1" in diameter

Tapestry needle

gauge:

22 sts and 26 rows to 4" (10cm) square measured over St st using size 5 (3.75mm) needles. Always work a gauge swatch and change needle size if necessary.

tips and techniques:

As the button and buttonhole bands are integral, do not join new balls of yarn at front edges, but join at side and armhole edges.

Fully fashioned shaping

Decreasing on a knit row:

K3, k2tog, k to last 5 sts, k2tog tbl, k3.

Decreasing on a purl row:

P3, p2tog tbl, p to last 5 sts, p2tog, p3.

Increasing on a knit row:

K3, M1, k to last 3 sts, M1, k3.

to knit the back:

Using size 3 (3.25mm) needles, cast on 118 (122, 130, 134, 142) sts and work in rib as follows:

Row 1 (RS) K2, [p2, k2] to end.

Row 2 P2, [k2, p2] to end.

Rep last 2 rows until work measures 2$\frac{3}{4}$" (7cm), ending with RS facing for next row and inc 0 (1, 0, 1, 0) st at each end of last row. **118 (124, 130, 136, 142) sts.**

Change to size 5 (3.75mm) needles and beg with a k row, work in St st until back measures 17 (17$\frac{1}{4}$, 17$\frac{1}{2}$, 17$\frac{3}{4}$, 18$\frac{1}{2}$)" (43 [44, 45, 46, 47])cm from cast-on edge, ending with RS facing for next row.

shape armholes

Bind off 6 sts at beg of next 2 rows. **106 (112, 118, 124, 130) sts.**

Dec 1 st (see note on fully fashioned shaping above) at each end of next 3 (3, 5, 5, 7) rows, then on foll 2 (2, 2, 4, 4) alt rows, then on 0 (2, 2, 2, 2) foll 4th rows. **96 (98, 100, 102, 104) sts rem.**

Work even until armhole measures 8$\frac{3}{4}$ (9, 9$\frac{1}{2}$, 9$\frac{3}{4}$,

10$\frac{1}{4}$" (22 [23, 24, 25, 26])cm, ending with RS facing for next row.

shape shoulders and back neck

Bind off 9 (10, 10, 11, 11) sts at beg of next 2 rows. **78 (78, 80, 80, 82) sts.**

Next row Bind off 9 (10, 10, 11, 11) sts, k until there are 16 (15, 15, 14, 14) sts on RH needle, turn and work on these sts only for first side of neck

Bind off 4 sts at beg of next row.

Bind off rem 12 (11, 11, 10, 10) sts.

With RS facing, rejoin yarn to rem sts, bind off center 28 (28, 30, 30, 32) sts and k to end of row.

Complete to match first side, reversing shaping.

to knit the right front:

Using size 3 (3.25mm) needles, cast on 67 (71, 75, 75, 79) sts and work as follows:

Row 1 (RS) [P1, k1] 4 times, p1, [k2, p2] to last 2 sts, k2.

Row 2 P2, [k2, p2] to last 9 sts, [k1, p1] 4 times, k1.

Rep last 2 rows until work measures 2$\frac{3}{4}$" (7cm), ending with RS facing for next row and inc 2 (1, 0, 3, 2) sts evenly across last row. **69 (72, 75, 78, 81) sts.**

Change to size 5 (3.75mm) needles and beg with a k row, work in St st with the 9-st single rib front band until work measures 16$\frac{1}{4}$ (16$\frac{1}{2}$, 16$\frac{3}{4}$, 17, 17$\frac{3}{4}$)" (41 [42, 43, 44, 45])cm, ending with RS facing for next row.

shape front slope

Next row [P1, k1] 4 times, p1, k3, k2tog, k to end.

Dec 1 st at neck edge in this way on foll 1 (2, 2, 1, 1) alt rows, then on every foll 3rd row (see note on fully fashioned shaping on a WS row. page 44), **and at the same time** when front matches Back to start of armhole shaping and with WS facing, shape armhole as follows:

shape armhole

Cont to dec at front edge and bind off 6 sts at beg of next row.

Work 1 row.

Dec 1 st at armhole edge on next 3 (3, 5, 5, 7) rows, then on foll 2 (2, 2, 4, 4) alt rows, then on 0 (2, 2, 2, 2) foll 4th rows.

Keeping armhole edge straight, cont to dec at front edge only until 39 (40, 40, 41, 41) sts rem.

Work even until armhole matches Back to start of shoulder shaping, ending with WS facing for next row.

shape shoulder

Next row Bind off 9 (10, 10, 11, 11) sts, p to last 9 sts, turn and leave rem 9 rib sts on a holder.

Work 1 row.

Bind off 9 (10, 10, 11, 11) sts at beg of next row.

Work 1 row.

Bind off rem 12 (11, 11, 10, 10) sts.

to knit the left front:

Using size 3 (3.25mm) needles, cast on 67 (71, 75, 75, 79) sts and work as follows:

Row 1 (RS) [K2, p2] to last 11 sts, k2, [p1, k1] 4 times, p1.

Row 2 [K1, p1] 4 times, k1, [p2, k2] to last 2 sts, p2.

Rep last 2 rows until work measures 1" (2.5cm) from cast-on edge, ending with RS facing for next row.

Buttonhole row (RS) [P1, k1] twice, yo, k2tog, p1, k1, p1, [k2, p2] to last 2 sts, k2.

Cont in rib as set until work measures 2$\frac{3}{4}$" (7cm), ending with RS facing for next row and inc 2 (1, 0, 3, 2) sts evenly across last row. **69 (72, 75, 78, 81) sts.**

Change to size 5 (3.75mm) needles and beg with a k row, work in St st with the 9-st single rib front band until work measures 16$\frac{1}{4}$ (16$\frac{1}{2}$, 16$\frac{3}{4}$, 17, 17$\frac{3}{4}$)" (41 [42, 43, 44, 45])cm from cast-on edge, making 4 more buttonholes in the rib band at 3$\frac{1}{2}$ (3$\frac{1}{2}$, 3$\frac{1}{2}$, 3$\frac{3}{4}$, 3$\frac{3}{4}$)" (9 [9, 9, 9.5, 9.5])cm intervals and ending with RS facing for next row.

shape front slope

Next row K to last 14 sts, k2tog tbl, k3, [p1, k1] 4 times, p1.

Now complete to match Right Front, reversing all shapings and working an extra row before beg of armhole and shoulder shapings.

to knit the sleeves:

Using size 3 (3.25mm) needles, cast on 54 (58, 58, 62, 62) sts and work 2$\frac{3}{4}$" (7cm) in rib as given for Back, ending with RS facing for next row.

Change to size 5 (3.75mm) needles.

Next row (RS) K3, M1, k to last 3 sts, M1, k3.

Beg with a p row, work in St st, inc 1 st at each end of every foll 8th row until there are 82 (84, 86, 88, 90) sts.

Work even until sleeve measures 18$\frac{1}{2}$ (19, 19, 19$\frac{1}{4}$,

s 42½" / 108cm
m 44¾" / 114cm
l 46¾" / 119cm
xl 49¼" / 125cm
xxl 51¼" / 130cm

s 18" / 47cm
m 19" / 48cm
l 19" / 48cm
xl 19¼" / 49cm
xxl 19¼" / 49cm

s 25¾" / 65cm
m 26¼" / 67cm
l 27" / 69cm
xl 28" / 71cm
xxl 28¾" / 73cm

19¼)" (47 [48, 48, 49, 49])cm from cast-on edge, ending with RS facing for next row.

shape top of sleeve

Bind off 6 sts at beg of next 2 rows. 70 (72, 74, 76, 78) sts.

Next row K3, k2tog, k to last 5 sts, k2tog tbl, k3.
Next row P3, p2tog tbl, p to last 5 sts, p2tog, p3.
Next row K3, k2tog, k to last 5 sts, k2tog tbl, k3.
Dec 1 st at each end of next 2 alt rows, then at each end of every foll 4th row until 56 (58, 60, 62, 64) sts rem.
Work 1 row.
Dec 1 st at each end of next row and foll 4 alt rows. 46 (48, 50, 52, 54) sts.
Dec 1 st at each end of next 9 rows. 28 (30, 32, 34, 36) sts.
Bind off 4 (4, 5, 5, 6) sts at beg of next 2 rows.
Bind off rem 20 (22, 22, 24, 24) sts.

to make up:

Weave in any yarn ends.
Lay pieces out flat on a towel or blanket and pin in position, easing work straight if necessary. Gently steam.

back neckband

Sew both shoulder seams.
Using size 5 (3.75mm) needles, slip 9 sts of right front band onto needle, rejoin yarn and cont in rib as set until band when slightly stretched, fits across back neck edge to reach 9 sts on left front band holder.
Graft 2 sets of 9 sts together.
Sew band to back neck edge.

to finish:

Sew sleeves into armholes, easing to fit.
Sew side and sleeve seams, using mattress stitch.
Sew on buttons.

SIMPLE VEST

A simple pullover knitted in natural silk cotton yarn. The V-neck and armhole edges are worked in with the body to give a neat but raw edge, so there is no additional picking up of stitches or ends to weave in. The rib stitch pattern, together with the texture of the tweed yarn, adds a little detail to this great basic. This versatile pullover looks equally good in a neutral shade or seasonal color.

sizes:

	s	m	l	xl	xxl	
to fit chest	36	38	40	42	44	inches
	92	97	102	107	112	cm
actual chest	38½	41¼	44	47¼	50	inches
	98	105	112	120	127	cm
actual length	24	24¾	25½	26¼	27	inches
	61	63	65	67	69	cm

materials:

6 (7, 8, 9, 10) hanks of Rowan Summer Tweed; 70% silk, 30% cotton; color gray or red; 1¾ oz (50g) 118yd (108m); (4) medium.

Sizes 7 and 8 (4.5mm and 5mm) needles

Tapestry needle

gauge:

16 sts and 23 rows to 4" (10cm) square measured over St st using size 8 (5mm) needles. Always work a gauge swatch and change needle size if necessary.

to knit the back:

Using size 7 (4.5mm) needles, cast on 80 (86, 92, 98, 104) sts and work in rib as follows:
Row 1 (RS) [P2, k1] to last 2 sts, p2.
Row 2 [K2, p1] to last 2 sts, p2.
Rep last 2 rows until work measures 2¼ (2¼, 2¾, 2¾, 3¼)" (6 [6, 7, 7, 8])cm, ending with RS facing for next row.
Change to size 8 (5mm) needles and work in patt

as follows:
Row 1 (RS) [P2, k1] 3 times, p2, k to last 11 sts, [p2, k1] 3 times, p2.
Row 2 [K2, p1] 3 times, k2, p to last 11 sts, [k2, p1] 3 times, k2.
These 2 rows form the St st with ribbed edges and are repeated.
Cont in patt as set until back measures 15¾ (16, 16½, 16¾, 17¼)" (40 [41, 42, 43, 44])cm from cast-on edge, ending with RS facing for next row.

shape armholes
Bind off 5 sts in rib at beg of next 2 rows, keeping rem rib sts as set. **70 (76, 82, 88, 94) sts.**
Next row (dec row) [K1, p2] twice, k2tog, k to last 8 sts, k2tog tbl, [p2, k1] twice.
Next row [P1, k2] twice, p to last 6 sts, [k2, p1] twice.
Rep last 2 rows 4 times more. **60 (66, 72, 78, 84) sts.**
Keeping rib edges as set, work even until armhole measures 8¼ (8¾, 9, 9½, 9¾)" (21 [22, 23, 24, 25])cm, ending with RS facing for next row.

shape shoulders and back neck
Bind off 4 (5, 6, 6, 6) sts at beg of next 4 rows. **44 (46, 48, 54, 60) sts.**
Next row Bind off 4 (4, 5, 6, 7) sts, k until there are 8 sts on RH needle, turn and work on these sts only for first side of neck.
Bind off 3 sts at beg (neck edge) of next row.
Bind off rem 5 sts.
With RS facing, rejoin yarn to rem sts, bind off center 20 (22, 24, 26, 28) sts and work to end of row.
Complete to match first side, reversing shaping.

to knit the front:

Work as given for Back until work measures 10½ (11¾, 13, 13¼, 13¾)" (27 [30, 33, 34, 35])cm from cast-on edge, ending with RS facing for next row.

Next row Rib 11 sts, k26 (29, 32, 35, 38) sts, p2, k2, p2, k to last 11 sts, rib to end.

Next row Rib 11 sts, p26 (29, 32, 35, 38) sts, k2, p2, k2, p to last 11 sts, rib to end.

Rep last 2 rows until work measures 12½ (13¾, 15, 15¼, 15¾)" (32 [35, 38, 39, 40])cm from cast-on edge, ending with RS facing for next row.

Next row Rib 11 sts, k23 (26, 29, 32, 35) sts, p2, k1, p2, k2, p2, k1, p2, k to last 11 sts, rib to end.

Next row Rib 11 sts, p23 (26, 29, 32, 37) sts, k2, p1, k2, p2, k2, p1, k2, p to last 11 sts, rib to end.

Rep last 2 rows until work measures 15¾ (16, 16½, 16¾, 17¼)" (40 [41, 42, 43, 44])cm from cast-on edge, ending with RS facing for next row.

shape armholes

Bind off 5 sts in rib at beg of next 2 rows, keeping rem rib sts as set. **70 (76, 82, 88, 94) sts.**

Next row (dec row) [K1, p2] twice, k2tog, work as set to last 8 sts, k2tog tbl, [p2, k1] twice.

Next row [P1, k2] twice, work as set to last 6 sts, [k2, p1] twice.

Rep last 2 rows 4 times more. **60 (66, 72, 78, 84) sts.**

Keeping rib center panel and edges as set, work even until front measures 17¾ (18, 18½, 18¾, 19¼)" (45 [46, 47, 48, 49])cm from cast-on edge, ending with RS facing for next row.

divide for neck

Next row Patt 30 (33, 36, 39, 42) sts, keeping ribbed armhole and neck edges correct, turn and leave rem sts on a holder.

Work each side of neck separately.

Next row Patt across sts as set.

shape neck

Next row (RS) Patt to last 8 sts, k2tog tbl, [p2, k1] twice.

Cont to dec 1 st at neck edge (6 sts in from edge) on every foll 4th (4th, 4th, 4th, 3rd) row until 23 (25, 28, 29, 30) sts rem.

Work even until armhole matches Back to start of shoulder shaping, ending with RS facing for next row.

shape shoulder

Bind off 4 (5, 6, 6, 6) sts at beg of next row and foll alt row.

Work 1 row.

Next row Bind off 4 (4, 5, 6, 7) sts, work to last 6 rib

sts, turn, leaving rib stitches on holder.

Work 1 row.

Bind off rem 5 sts.

With RS facing, rejoin yarn to rem sts and work across sts as set.

Complete to match first side reversing shaping.

to finish:

Weave in any yarn ends.

Lay work out flat and gently steam.

back neckband

Sew both shoulder seams.

Using size 7 (4.5mm) needles, slip 6 sts from right shoulder holder back onto needle, rejoin yarn and cont in rib as set until band fits across back neck, slightly stretching to reach sts on left shoulder holder.

Graft 2 sets of sts together.

Sew band to back neck edge.

Sew side seams.

s 38½" / 98cm
m 41¼" / 105cm
l 44" / 112cm
xl 47¼" / 120cm
xxl 50" / 127cm

s 24" / 61cm
m 24¾" / 63cm
l 25½" / 65cm
xl 26¼" / 67cm
xxl 27" / 69cm

casual favorites

HAND-DYED SWEATER

Knit on large needles and worked into a strong sweater shape, each stitch of this super-bulky yarn helps create a pattern. Luxurious alpaca has been blended with soft wool into a highly individual yarn, which is kettle dyed to add a further color dimension. Vibrant and naturally variegated tones are achieved in this way, with each hank of yarn a unique creation. By keeping the design simple, the yarn is truly showcased to maximum effect.

sizes:

	s	m	l	xl	xxl	
to fit chest	36	38	40	42	44	inches
	92	97	102	107	112	cm
actual chest	47¼	49¼	51½	54	56	inches
	120	125	131	137	142	cm
actual length	25¼	26¼	27½	28¾	30	inches
	64	67	70	73	76	cm
sleeve length	18	18½	18½	19	19	inches
	46	47	47	48	48	cm

materials:

15 (15, 16, 16, 17) hanks of Blue Sky Alpacas Hand-dyed Bulky Alpaca; 50% alpaca, 50% wool; color brown or turquoise; 3½ oz (100g) 98yd (90m); (6) superbulky.

Size size 17 (12mm) needles

2 stitch holders or safety pins

Tapestry needle

gauge:

7 sts and 11 rows to 4" (10cm) square measured over St st using size 17 (12mm) needles. Always work a gauge swatch and change needle size if necessary.

to knit the back:

Cast on 44 (46, 48, 50, 52) sts.
Rib row [K1, p1] to end.
This row forms rib and is repeated.
Work 2½ (2½, 2½, 3, 3)" (6.5 [6.5, 6.5, 7.5, 7.5])cm in rib.
Work in St st until work measures 16½ (17¼, 18, 19, 19¾)" (42 [44, 46, 48, 50])cm from cast-on edge, ending with RS facing for next row.

shape armhole

Bind off 2 sts at beg of next 2 rows. 40 (42, 44, 46, 48) sts.
Next row K3, skp, k to last 5 sts, k2tog, k3.
P 1 row.
Rep last 2 rows once more. 36 (38, 40, 42, 44) sts.
Work even until armhole measures 8¾ (9, 9½, 9¾, 10¼)" (22 [23, 24, 25, 26])cm, ending with RS facing for next row.

shape shoulders and back neck

Bind off 3 sts at beg next 2 rows.
Next row Bind off 3 (4, 4, 5, 5) sts, k until there are 7 (7, 8, 8, 8) sts on RH needle, turn and leave rem sts on a holder.
Bind off 3 sts at beg of next row.
Bind off rem 4 (4, 5, 5, 5) sts.
With RS facing, rejoin yarn to rem stitches on holder, bind off center 10 (10, 10, 10, 12) sts and k to end of row.
Complete to match first side, reversing shaping.

to knit the front:

Work as given for Back until 8 (8, 8, 8, 10) rows less have been worked to start of shoulder shaping, ending with RS facing for next row.

shape neck

Next row (RS) K15 (16, 17, 18, 19) sts, turn and leave rem sts on a holder.

Work each side separately.

Dec 1 st (3 sts from edge) at neck edge on next 4 rows, then on following 1 (1, 1, 1, 2) alt rows. **10 (11, 12, 13, 13) sts.**

Work even for 1 row, ending with RS facing for next row.

shape shoulder

Bind off 3 sts at beg of next row and 3 (4, 4, 5, 5) sts at beg of foll alt row.

Work 1 row.

Bind off rem 4 (4, 5, 5, 5) sts.

With RS facing, rejoin yarn to rem sts, bind off center 6 sts and k to end of row.

Complete to match first side reversing shaping.

to knit the sleeves:

Cast on 20 (22, 22, 24, 26) sts and work 3¼" (8cm) in k1, p1 rib as given for Back, ending with RS facing for next row.

Inc row K3, M1, k to last 3 sts, M1, k3.

Cont in St st, inc 1 st as before at each end of 4 foll 8th rows.

30 (32, 32, 34, 36) sts.

Work even until sleeve measures 18 (18½, 18½, 19, 19)" (46 [47, 47, 48, 48])cm from cast-on edge, ending with RS facing for next row.

shape top of sleeve

Bind off 2 sts at beg next 2 rows.

26 (28, 28, 30, 32) sts.

Dec row K3, skp, k to last 5 sts, k2tog, k3.

P 1 row.

Dec 1 st as before at each end of next row and foll 4th row, then on every alt row until 10 (12, 12, 12, 12) sts rem.

Next row P3, p2tog tbl, p0 (2, 2, 2, 2), p2tog, p3.
Bind off.

to make the collar:

Cast on 46 (46, 46, 50, 50) sts and work 3½" (9cm) in k1, p1 rib.

Bind off loosely in rib.

to finish:

Weave in all yarn ends.

Graft shoulder seams.

Sew sleeves into armholes, easing to fit.

Fold work in half and sew sleeve and side seams, using mattress stitch.

Sew row ends of collar together and with seam to center back, ease collar around the neck edge and sew in position.

s 18" / 46cm
m 18½" / 47cm
l 18½" / 47cm
xl 19" / 48cm
xxl 19" / 48cm

s 47¼" / 120cm
m 49¼" / 125cm
l 51½" / 131cm
xl 54" / 137cm
xxl 56" / 142cm

s 25¼" / 64cm
m 26¼" / 67cm
l 27½" / 70cm
xl 28¾" / 73cm
xxl 30" / 76cm

MULTI-STRIPE SWEATER

A colorful slim-fit sweater worked in a random sequence of stripes. Anchored by shades of light gray, stone, and navy blue, it goes well with casual wear. On the sleeves, the rib is carried halfway down from the deep raglan and then switches to reverse stockinette stitch. A simple self-stripe collar finishes off the design. The sweater is worked in an medium-weight yarn of a soft extra-fine merino wool and cashmere blend making this a very comfortable item.

sizes:

	s	m	l	xl	xxl	
to fit chest	36	38	40	42	44	inches
	92	97	102	107	112	cm
actual chest	41¼	43¼	44¾	46½	48	inches
	105	110	114	118	122	cm
actual length	25½	26¼	26¾	27½	28¼	inches
	65	67	68	70	72	cm
sleeve length	18½	19	19	19¼	19¼	inches
	47	48	48	49	49	cm

materials:

4 balls of Debbie Bliss Cashmerino Aran; 55% merino wool, 33% microfiber, 12% cashmere; 1¾oz (50g) 98yd (90m); (4) medium in each of beige (A) and navy (B), 3 balls in each of teal (C) and denim (G), and 2 balls in each of grape (D), light teal (E), and silver (F).

Sizes 7 and 8 (4.5mm and 5mm) needles

2 stitch holders or safety pins

Tapestry needle

gauge:

18 sts and 24 rows measured over St st and 20 sts and 24 rows measured over rib patt, both to 4" (10cm) square using size 8 (5mm) needles. Always work a gauge swatch and change needle size if necessary.

tips and techniques:

Weave in the yarn ends on the wrong side of the work as you knit. When working the reverse St st section of the sleeves and weaving in yarn ends, remember that the wrong side is the knit side of the work.

color sequence:

5 rows B.
1 row C.
2 rows A.
1 row B.
4 rows D.
1 row E.
3 rows F.
2 rows B.
6 rows C.
1 row B.
1 row E.
1 row G.
1 row E.
1 row A.
1 row F.
1 row A.
1 row C.
4 rows A.
1 row D.
2 rows A.
1 row F.
8 rows G.
1 row A.

to knit the back:

Using size 7 (4.5mm) needles and B, cast on 107 (112, 117, 122, 127) sts.
Working color sequence throughout, work in rib as follows:
Row 1 (RS) [K3, p2] to last 2 sts, k2.
Row 2 P2, [k2, p3] to end of row.
Repeat last 2 rows 4 times more.
Change to size 8 (5mm) needles and cont in rib as set until work measures 14$\frac{1}{2}$ (15, 15, 15$\frac{1}{4}$, 15$\frac{1}{4}$)" (37 [38, 38, 39, 39])cm from cast-on edge, ending with RS facing for next row.

shape raglans
Bind off 4 sts at beg of next 2 rows. 99 (104, 109, 114, 119) sts.
Next row (dec row) K3, p2tog, p1, rib as set to last 6 sts, p1, p2tog, k3.
Next row P3, k2, rib to last 5 sts, k2, p3. **
Rep last 2 rows until 33 (36, 37, 40, 41) sts rem.
Bind off.

to knit the front:

Work as given for Back to **.
Rep last 2 rows until 44 (46, 46, 48, 48) sts rem, ending with RS facing for next row.

shape neck
Next row K3, p2tog, p1, rib 6 sts as set, turn and leave rem sts on a holder.
Work each side of neck separately.
Dec 1 st at neck edge on next 2 rows, then on foll 3 alt rows, **and at the same time** cont to dec at raglan edge on every RS row until 2 sts rem.
Work 1 row.
Next row K2tog and fasten off.
With RS facing, slip center 19 (22, 23, 26, 27) sts onto a holder, rejoin yarn to rem sts, rib as set to last 6 sts, p1, p2tog, k3.
Complete to match first side, reversing shaping.

to knit the sleeves:

Using size 7 (4.5mm) needles and B, cast on 52 sts for all sizes.
Working color sequence throughout, work in rib as follows:
Row 1 (RS) P2, [k3, p2] to end.
Row 2 K2, [p3, k2] to end.
Rep last 2 rows until work measures 3" (7.5cm), ending with RS facing for next row.
Change to size 8 (5mm) needles.
Beg with a p row, work in rev St st, inc 1 st at each end of 5th and every foll 6th row until there are 78 sts, taking inc sts into rib patt.
Work even for 8 rows, ending with WS facing for next row.
Next row K and inc 5 sts evenly across row. 83 sts.
Now work in rib patt as follows:
Next row (RS) K3, [p2, k3] to end of row.
Next row P3, [k2, p3] to end of row.
Cont in rib as set until sleeve measures 18$\frac{1}{2}$ (19, 19, 19$\frac{1}{4}$, 19$\frac{1}{4}$)" (47 [48, 48, 49, 49])cm from cast-on edge, ending with RS facing for next row.

shape raglan
Keeping rib correct, bind off 4 sts at beg of next 2 rows. 75 sts.
Working all decs as given for Back raglan, dec 1 st at each end of next and every foll 4th row until 63 (61, 59,

s 41¼" / 105cm
m 43¼" / 110cm
l 44¾" / 114cm
xl 46½" / 118cm
xxl 48" / 122cm

s 18½" / 47cm
m 19" / 48cm
l 19" / 48cm
xl 19¼" / 49cm
xxl 19¼" / 49cm

s 25½" / 65cm
m 26¼" / 67cm
l 26¾" / 68cm
xl 27½" / 70cm
xxl 28¼" / 72cm

55, 51) sts rem, then on every foll RS row until 19 sts rem, ending with WS facing for next row.
Next row P3, k2tog, k1, k2tog, p3, k2tog, k1, k2tog, p3. **15 sts.**
Bind off.

to make the collar:

Sew both front raglan seams and right back raglan seam, using mattress stitch.

With RS facing, size 7 (4.5mm) needles, and B, pick up and k 15 sts from top of left sleeve, 8 sts down left front neck, 19 (22, 23, 26, 27) sts from center front holder, 8 sts up right front neck, 15 sts from top of right sleeve and 32 (34, 38, 40, 39) sts across back neck. **97 (102, 107, 112, 112) sts.**

Beg with 1st row of color sequence, work in rib as follows:

Row 1 (WS) K2, [p3, k2] to end of row.
Row 2 P2, [k3, p2] to end of row.
Rep last 2 rows until work measures 3 (3, 3¼, 3¼, 3½)" (7.5 [7.5, 8.5, 8.5, 9])cm.
Bind off loosely but evenly in rib.

to finish:

Weave in any yarn ends.
Lay work out flat and gently steam, taking care not to press and flatten the rib patt.
Sew remaining raglan and collar seams, using mattress stitch and matching stripes.
Sew the sleeve and side seams, again taking care to match the colors and stripes.

FAVORITE SWEATSHIRT

A sweatshirt-style sweater knit in versatile hemp yarn with external seam detailing. Worked in simple stockinette stitch and reverse stockinette stitch, this garment is seamed visibly on the outside of the sweater to give it a "deconstructed" look.

sizes:

	s	m	l	xl	xxl	
to fit chest	36	38	40	42	44	inches
	92	97	102	107	112	cm
actual chest	42	43¾	44¾	46½	48	inches
	107	111	114	118	122	cm
actual length	24½	25¾	26¾	28	29	inches
	62	65	68	71	74	cm
sleeve length	17¾	18½	19¼	20	20¾	inches
	45	47	49	51	53	cm

materials:

9 (10, 10, 11, 11) skeins of Lanaknits Hemp for Knitting Allhemp6; 100% hemp; colour navy; 3½ oz (100g) 165yd (150m); 🎞3 light.

Sizes 3 and 5 (3.25mm and 3.75mm) needles

Tapestry needle

gauge:

22 sts and 28 rows to 4" (10cm) square measured over St st using size 5 (3.75mm) needles. Always work a gauge swatch and change needle size if necessary.

tips and techniques:

The back, front, and sleeves are all made in two sections (the lower section in rev St st and the upper section in St st), which are sewn together with an external seam.

Fully fashioned shaping

Decreasing on a knit row:

K3, k2tog, k to last 5 sts, k2tog tbl, k3.

Decreasing on a purl row:

P3, p2tog tbl, p to last 5 sts, p2tog, p3.

Increasing on a knit row:

K3, M1, k to last 3 sts, M1, k3.

s 42" / 107cm
m 43³/₄" / 111cm
l 44³/₄" / 114cm
xl 46¹/₂" / 118cm
xxl 48" / 122cm

s 17³/₄" / 45cm
m 18¹/₂" / 47cm
l 19¹/₄" / 49cm
xl 20" / 51cm
xxl 20³/₄" / 53cm

s 24¹/₂" / 62cm
m 25³/₄" / 65cm
l 26³/₄" / 68cm
xl 28" / 71cm
xxl 29" / 74cm

to knit the back:

lower section

Using size 3 (3.25mm) needles, cast on 120 (124, 128, 132, 136) sts.

Rib row [K1, p1] to end.

This row forms rib and is repeated.

Work 3¹/₄" (8cm) in rib.

Change to size 5 (3.75mm) needles and beg with a RS (p) row, work in rev St st until work measures 10¹/₂ (11, 11¹/₄, 11³/₄, 12)" (27 [28, 29, 30, 31])cm from cast-on edge, ending with RS facing for next row.

Bind off firmly.

upper section

Using size 5 (3.75mm) needles, cast on 120 (124, 128, 132, 136) sts and beg with a RS (k) row, work in St st until work measures 5¹/₂ (6, 6¹/₄, 6³/₄, 7)" (14 [15, 16, 17, 18])cm from cast-on edge, ending with RS facing for next row.

shape armholes

Bind off 6 sts at beg of next 2 rows. 108 (112, 116, 120, 124) sts.

Dec 1 st (see notes on fully fashioned shaping, page 68)

at each end of next 3 rows, then on foll 2 RS rows. 98 (102, 106, 110, 114) sts. **

Work even until armhole measures 8³/₄ (9, 9¹/₂, 9³/₄, 10¹/₄)" (22 [23, 24, 25, 26])cm ending with RS facing for next row.

shape back neck and shoulders

Next row Bind off 13 (14, 15, 16, 17) sts, k until there are 18 sts on RH needle, turn and work on these sts only for first side of neck.

Next row Bind off 4 sts, p to end of row.

Bind off rem 14 sts.

With RS facing, rejoin yarn to rem sts, bind off center 36 (38, 40, 42, 44) sts and k to end of row.

Complete to match first side, reversing shaping.

to knit the front:

lower section

Work as given for lower section of Back.

upper section

Work as given for upper section of Back to **.

Work even until armhole measures 6³/₄ (7, 7¹/₂, 7³/₄,

8¼)" (17 [18, 19, 20, 21])cm, ending with RS facing for next row.

shape neck

Next row K41 (42, 43, 44, 45) sts, turn and work on these sts only for first side of neck.

Bind off 6 sts at beg of next row. 35 (36, 37, 38, 39) sts.

Dec 1 st (see notes on fully fashioned shaping, page 68) at neck edge on next 6 rows, then on foll 2 RS rows. 27 (28, 29, 30, 31) sts.

Work even until armhole matches Back to shoulder, ending at armhole edge.

Bind off 13 (14, 15, 16, 17) sts at beg of next row.

Work 1 row.

Bind off rem 14 sts.

With RS facing, rejoin yarn to rem sts, bind off center 16 (18, 20, 22, 24) sts and work to end of row.

Complete to match first side, reversing shaping.

to knit the sleeves:

lower section

Using size 3 (3.25mm) needles, cast on 50 (52, 52, 54, 56) sts and work 3¼" (8cm) in k1, p1 rib as given for Back.

Change to size 5 (3.75mm) needles and beg with a RS (p) row, work in rev St st, inc 1 st (see notes on fully fashioned shaping, page 68) at each end of 5th and every foll 6th row until work measures 10½ (11, 11¼, 11¾, 12)" (27 [28, 29, 30, 31])cm from cast-on edge, ending with RS facing for next row.

Bind off firmly.

upper section

Cast on the same number of sts bound off from lower section and beg with a RS (k) row, work in St st and cont to inc as set until there are 84 (88, 88, 92, 96) sts.

Work even until upper section measures 7½ (7¾, 8¼,

8½, 9)" (19 [20, 21, 22, 23])cm from cast-on edge, ending with RS facing for next row.

shape top of sleeve

Bind off 6 sts at beg of next 2 rows. 72 (76, 76, 80, 84) sts.

Dec 1 st at each end of next 3 rows. 66 (70, 70, 74, 78) sts.

Dec 1 st at each end of every foll RS row until 32 (34, 36, 40, 44) sts rem, ending with RS facing for next row.

Bind off 6 (7, 7, 8, 9) sts at beg of next 2 rows. 20 (20, 22, 24, 26) sts.

Bind off rem 20 (20, 22, 24, 26) sts.

to knit the collar:

Using size 3 (3.25mm) needles, cast on 100 (104, 108, 112, 116) sts and beg with a RS (k) row, work 2¾" (7cm) in St st.

Bind off.

to finish:

Weave in any yarn ends.

Lay pieces out flat on a towel or blanket and pin in position, easing work straight if necessary. Gently steam.

Sew together lower and upper sections of Back, making an external seam with backstitch.

Sew together front and sleeve sections in the same way.

Graft shoulder seams.

Sew together row ends of collar, then using backstitch, sew cast-on edge of collar inside neck edge, so making an external seam.

Sew sleeves into armholes, easing to fit.

Sew side and sleeve seams from armhole to cuff edge and hem, using mattress stitch.

HERRINGBONE SWEATER

Herringbone fabric is a perennial classic for men's suits. Here, this traditional pattern has been worked into a simple jacquard stitch. The sweater is knit in luxurious baby alpaca yarn, so even though it looks very urban it is still quite soft.

sizes:

	s	m	l	xl	xxl	
to fit chest	36	38	40	42	44	inches
	92	97	102	107	112	cm
actual chest	40½	42½	44½	46½	48½	inches
	103	108	113	118	123	cm
actual length	25¼	26	26¾	27½	28¼	inches
	64	66	68	70	72	cm
sleeve length	19	19¼	19¾	20	20½	inches
	48	49	50	51	52	cm

materials:

8 (8, 9, 9, 10) balls of Rowan Classic Baby Alpaca DK; 100% baby alpaca; 1¾oz (50g) 109yd (100m); **(3)** light, in each of light gray (A) and dark gray (B).

Sizes 5 and 7 (3.75mm and 4.5mm) needles

Tapestry needle

gauge:

24 sts and 22 rows to 4" (10cm) square measured over herringbone pattern using size 7 (4.5mm) needles. Always work a gauge swatch and change needle size if necessary.

tips and techniques:

Fully fashioned shaping
Decreasing on a knit row:
K1, k2tog, patt to last 3 sts, k2tog tbl, k1.
Decreasing on a purl row:
P1, p2tog tbl, patt to last 3 sts, p2tog, p1.
Increasing on a knit row:
K1, M1, patt to last st, M1, k1.

herringbone pattern:

Worked over a multiple of 6 sts.
Work in St st, using A and B as follows:
Row 1 (RS) K all sts, working [2A, 1B] to end of row.
Row 2 P all sts, working [1A, 1B, 3A, 1B] to end of row.
Row 3 K all sts, working 1A, 1B [1A, 1B, 3A, 1B] to last 4 sts, then 1A, 1B, 2A.
Row 4 P all sts, working [1B, 2A] to end of row.
Row 5 K all sts, working 1B, 3A [1B, 1A, 1B, 3A] to last 2 sts, then 1B, 1A.
Row 6 P all sts, working 2A, 1B, 1A, 1B [3A, 1B, 1A, 1B] to last st, then 1A.
These 6 rows form the herringbone pattern and are repeated throughout.

to knit the back:

Using size 5 (3.75mm) needles and B, cast on 125 (131, 137, 143, 149) sts and work in rib as follows:

Row 1 (RS) K2, [p1, k2] to end of row.

Row 2 P2, [k1, p2] to end of row.

Rep last 2 rows until work measures 2¼ (2¼, 2¼, 2¾, 2¾)" (6 [6, 6, 7, 7])cm from cast-on edge, ending with RS facing for next row and inc 1 st on last row. 126 (132, 138, 144, 150) sts.

Change to size 7 (4.5mm) needles and work in herringbone patt (as given on page 74) until work measures 16½ (17, 17¼, 17¾, 18)" (42 [43, 44, 45, 46])cm from cast-on edge, ending with RS facing for next row.

shape armholes

Keeping patt correct, bind off 5 sts at beg of next 2 rows. 116 (122, 128, 134, 140) sts.

Dec 1 st at each end of next 3 rows, then on foll 2 RS rows, now dec 1 st at each end of 2 foll 4th rows. 102 (108, 114, 120, 126) sts. **

Work even until armhole measures 8¾ (9, 9½, 9¾, 10¼)" (22 [23, 24, 25, 26])cm, ending with RS facing for next row.

shape shoulders and back neck

Keeping patt correct, bind off 9 (9, 10, 11, 12) sts at beg of next 2 rows. 84 (90, 94, 98, 102) sts.

Next row Bind off 9 (10, 11, 11, 12) sts, work until there are 13 (14, 15, 16, 17) sts on RH needle, turn and leave rem sts on a holder.

Bind off 4 sts at beg of next row.

Bind off rem 9 (10, 11, 12, 13) sts.

With RS facing, slip center 40 (42, 42, 44, 44) sts onto a holder, rejoin yarn to rem sts and patt to end of row. Complete to match first side, reversing shaping.

to knit the front:

Work as given for Back to **.

Work even until armhole measures 2¾" (7cm), ending with RS facing for next row.

divide for neck

Next row Patt 51 (54, 57, 60, 63) sts, turn and leave rem sts on a holder.

Work 1 row.

Keeping patt correct, dec 1 st (see notes on fully fashioned shaping, page 74) at neck edge on next row and every foll row until 27 (29, 32, 34, 37) sts rem.

Work even until armhole measures 8¾ (9, 9½, 9¾, 10¼)" (22 [23, 24, 25, 26])cm, ending RS facing for next row.

shape shoulder

Keeping patt correct, bind off 9 (9, 10, 11, 12) sts at beg of next row.

Work 1 row.

Bind off 9 (10, 11, 11, 12) sts at beg of next row.

Work 1 row.

Bind off rem 9 (10, 11, 12, 13) sts.

With RS facing, rejoin yarn to rem sts and patt to end of row.

Work 1 row.

Complete to match first side, reversing shaping.

to knit the sleeves:

Using size 5 (3.75mm) needles and B, cast on 59 (59, 65, 65, 71) sts and work in rib as given for Back for 2¼" (6cm), ending with RS facing for next row and inc 1 st on last row. 60 (60, 66, 66, 72) sts.

Change to size 7 (4.5mm) needles and work in herringbone patt (as given on page 74), inc 1 st each end of 3rd and every foll 4th row until there are 70 (70, 76, 76, 82) sts, then on every foll 6th row until there are 92 (92, 98, 98, 104) sts.

Work even until sleeve measures 19 (19¼, 19¾, 20, 20½)" (48 [49, 50, 51, 52])cm from cast-on edge, ending with RS facing for next row.

shape top of sleeve

Keeping patt correct, bind off 5 sts at beg of next 2 rows. 82 (82, 88, 88, 94) sts.

Dec 1 st at each end of next 5 rows, then on foll 9 (9, 10, 10, 11) RS rows, then on next 10 rows. 34 (34, 38, 38, 42) sts.

Work 1 row.

Bind off 6 (6, 7, 7, 8) sts at beg of next 2 rows.

Bind off rem 22 (22, 24, 24, 26) sts.

s 19" / 48cm
m 19¼" / 49cm
l 19¾" / 50cm
xl 20" / 51cm
xxl 20½" / 52cm

s 40½" / 103cm
m 42½" / 108cm
l 44½" / 113cm
xl 46½" / 118cm
xxl 48½" / 123cm

s 25¼" / 64cm
m 26" / 66cm
l 26¾" / 68cm
xl 27½" / 70cm
xxl 28¼" / 72cm

to make the neckband:

Graft right shoulder seam.

With RS facing, size 5 (3.75mm) needles, and B, pick up and k 40 (42, 42, 44, 44) sts down left front neck, k into back of horizontal thread lying between 2 sts at center front and mark this st with a colored thread, pick up and k 40 (42, 42, 44, 44) sts up right front neck, 3 sts down right back neck, k across 40 (42, 42, 44, 44) sts at center back, then pick up and k 3 sts up left back neck. 127 (133, 133, 139, 139) sts.

Next row (WS) P1 (0, 0, 0, 0), k1 (0, 0, 1, 1), [p2, k1] to marked st, p1, [k1, p2] to last 1 (0, 0, 2, 2) sts, k1 (0, 0, 1, 1), p0 (0, 0, 1, 1).

Next row (RS) Rib as set to 2 sts before marked stitch, p2tog, k1, p2tog tbl, rib as set to end.

Next row Rib as set.

Rep last 2 rows until neckband measures 1¼" (3cm), ending with RS facing for next row.

Bind off in rib.

to finish:

Weave in any yarn ends.

Lay work out flat and gently steam each piece.

Graft left shoulder seam and sew neckband seam.

Sew sleeves into armholes, easing to fit.

Sew side and sleeve seams from armhole to cuff edge and hem, using mattress stitch.

COLLEGIATE CARDIGAN

A sumptuous shawl-collar cardigan made in a bulky-weight and ultra-soft cashmere merino blend yarn. The traditional Aran patterns used here are updated by supersizing the cables. This classic design has a wide integral collar and side pockets, and the wide rib button bands are worked in with the main body so there is very little finishing to do—just add a few seams and some great buttons!

sizes:

	s/m	m/l	xl/xxl	
to fit chest	36–38	38–40	42–44	inches
	92–97	97–102	107–112	cm
actual chest	44	46$\frac{1}{2}$	48	inches
	112	118	122	cm
actual length	26$\frac{1}{4}$	27$\frac{1}{2}$	28$\frac{3}{4}$	inches
	67	70	73	cm
sleeve length	19	19$\frac{3}{4}$	20$\frac{1}{2}$	inches
	48	50	52	cm

materials:

17 (18, 19) balls of Debbie Bliss Cashmerino Superchunky; 55% merino wool, 33% microfiber, 12% cashmere; color stone; 3$\frac{1}{2}$oz (100g) 82yd (75m); (5) bulky.

Sizes 10$\frac{1}{2}$ and 11 (7mm and 7.5mm) needles

Cable needle

5 natural horn buttons, 1" in diameter

gauge:

12 sts and 17 rows to 4" (10cm) square measured over St st using size 11 (7.5mm) needles. Always work a gauge swatch and change needle size if necessary.

tips and techniques:

Fully fashioned shaping
Decreasing on a knit row:
K1, k2tog, patt to last 3 sts, k2tog tbl, k1.
Decreasing on a purl row:
P1, p2tog tbl, patt to last 3 sts, p2tog, p1.
Increasing on a knit row:
K1, M1, patt to last st, M1, k1.

special abbreviations:

C10B slip 5 sts onto cable needle and hold at back of work, k5 from LH needle, then k5 from cable needle.
C10F slip next 5 sts onto cable needle and hold at front of work, k5 from LH needle, then k5 from cable needle.
C9F slip next 4 sts onto cable needle and hold at front of work, k5 from LH needle, then k4 from cable needle.
Tw2R k into front of second stitch on LH needle, then k the first st slipping both sts off LH needle together.

pattern A:

Worked over 20 sts and 12 rows.

Row 1 (RS) K.

Row 2 P.

Row 3 C10B, C10F.

Rows 5, 7, 9, and 11 Rep row 1.

Rows 4, 6, 8, 10, and 12 Rep row 2.

These 12 rows form Patt A and are repeated.

pattern B:

Worked over 9 sts and 18 rows.

Row 1 (RS) K.

Row 2 P.

Rows 3, 5, 7, 11, 13, 15, and 17 Rep row 1.

Rows 4, 6, 8, 10, 12, 14, 16, and 18 Rep row 2.

Row 9 C9F.

These 18 rows form Patt B and are repeated.

to knit the back:

Using size 10½ (7mm) needles, cast on 74 (78, 82) sts
and work in rib as follows:

Row 1 (RS) [K2 (1, 1), p1] 1 (1, 2) times, [k2, p1] to last
2 (1, 3) sts, k2 (1, 1), p0 (0, 1), k0 (0, 1).

Row 2 [P2 (1, 1), k1] 1 (1, 2) times, [p2, k1] to last
2 (1, 3) sts, p2 (1, 1), k0 (0, 1), p0 (0, 1).

Rep last 2 rows until work measures 1½ (1½, 2)"
(4 [4, 5])cm, ending with RS facing for next row.

Change to size 11 (7.5mm) needles and work in patt
as follows:

Row 1 (inc row) (RS) [K1, p1] 4 (5, 6) times, Tw2R, p3,
[inc in next st, k1] 6 times, inc in next st, p3, Tw2R, p3,
[k1, inc in next st] 3 times, p3, Tw2R, p3, [inc in next st,
k1] 6 times, inc in next st, p3, Tw2R, [k1, p1] 4 (5, 6)
times. **91 (95, 99) sts.**

Row 2 [P1, k1] 4 (5, 6) times, p2, k3, work row 2 of
Patt A, k3, p2, k3, work row 2 of Patt B, k3, p2, k3,
work row 2 of Patt A, k3, p2, [p1, k1] 4 (5, 6) times.

Row 3 [P1, k1] 4 (5, 6) times, Tw2R, p3, work row 3
of Patt A, p3, Tw2R, p3, work row 3 of Patt B, p3,
Tw2R, p3, work row 3 of Patt A, p3, Tw2R, [p1, k1]
4 (5, 6) times.

Row 4 [K1, p1] 4 (5, 6) times, p2, k3, work row 4 of
Patt A, k3, p2, k3, work row 4 of Patt B, k3, p2, k3,

work row 4 of Patt A, k3, p2, [k1, p1] 4 (5, 6) times.

Row 5 [K1, p1] 4 (5, 6) times, Tw2R, p3, work row 5 of
Patt A, p3, Tw2R, p3, work row 5 of Patt B, p3, Tw2R, p3,
work row 5 of Patt A, p3, Tw2R, [k1, p1] 4 (5, 6) times.

The last 4 rows set the position of the patt panels and
form the twisted sts and moss st at each side.

Working correct patt panel rows, cont in patt as set until
back measures 16¾ (17¼, 17¾)" (43 [44, 45])cm from
cast-on edge, placing colored markers at each end of
row 26 (for pocket placement) and ending with RS
facing for next row.

shape armholes

Keeping patt correct, bind off 3 sts at beg of next
2 rows. **85 (89, 93) sts.**

Dec 1 st at each end of next row and foll 2 alt rows.
79 (83, 87) sts.

Work even in patt until armhole measures 9½ (10¼,
11)" (24 [26, 28])cm, ending with WS facing for next row.

Dec row (WS) Patt 7 (9, 11), [p2tog, p1] 6 times, p2tog,
k3, p2, k3, [p1, p2tog] 3 times, k3, p2, k3, [p2tog, p1]
6 times, p2tog, patt to end. **62 (66, 70) sts.**

shape shoulders and back neck

Next row (RS) Bind off 9 (10, 10) sts, patt until there
are 11 (12, 12) sts on RH needle, turn and leave rem sts
on a holder.

Bind off 2 sts at beg of next row.

Bind off rem 9 (10, 10) sts.

With RS facing, rejoin yarn to rem sts on holder, bind off
center 22 (22, 24) sts at center back and patt to end
of row.

Complete to match first side, reversing shaping.

to knit the right front:

Using size 10½ (7mm) needles, cast on 47 (49, 51) sts
and work in rib as follows:

Row 1 (RS) [K1, p1] 6 times, [k2, p1] to last 2 (1, 3) sts,
k2 (1, 1), p0 (0, 1), k0 (0, 1).

Row 2 [P2 (1, 1), k1] 1 (1, 2) times, [p2, k1] to last
14 sts, p2, [k1, p1] 6 times.

Rep last 2 rows until work measures 1½ (1½, 2)"
(4 [4, 5])cm, ending with RS facing for next row.

Change to size 11 (7.5mm) needles and work as follows:

Row 1 (inc row) (RS) [K1, p1] 6 times, p3, Tw2R, p3,
[k1, inc in next st] 6 times, k2, p3, Tw2R, k1, [p1, k1]

2 (3, 4) times, k1, p1, k1. **53 (55, 57) sts.**

Row 2 P1, k1, p1, [p1, k1] 2 (3, 4) times, p3, k3, work row 2 of Patt A, k3, p2, k3, [k1, p1] 6 times.

Row 3 [K1, p1] 6 times, p3, Tw2R, p3, work row 3 of Patt A, p3, Tw2R, [p1, k1] 4 (5, 6) times.

Row 4 [P1, k1] 4 (5, 6) times, p2, k3, work row 4 of Patt A, k3, p2, k3, [k1, p1] 6 times.

Row 5 [K1, p1] 6 times, p3, Tw2R, p3, work row 5 of Patt A, p3, Tw2R, k1, [p1, k1] 2 (3, 4) times, k1, p1, k1.

The last 4 rows set the position of the pattern panel and form the twisted sts, 12-st front ribbed band, 5 (7, 9) sts in moss st at side, and 3-st ribbed pocket edging.

Working correct patt panel rows, work even in patt as set until front measures 6" (15.5cm) from cast-on edge, ending with RS facing for next row.

Next row Patt as set, but work last 8 (10, 12) sts in moss stitch.

Work even in patt until front measures 16$\frac{1}{4}$ (16$\frac{3}{4}$, 17$\frac{1}{4}$)" (42 [43, 44])cm from cast-on edge, ending with WS facing for next row.

shape front slope

Next row (WS) Patt to last 12 sts, turn and leave these sts on a holder for collar.

Dec 1 st (see notes on fully fashioned decreasing, page 80) at neck edge on next row and every foll 3rd row until 24 (26, 28) sts rem, then on every foll alt row until 18 (20, 22) sts rem, **and at the same time** when work measures 16$\frac{3}{4}$ (17$\frac{1}{4}$, 17$\frac{3}{4}$)" (43 [44, 45])cm from cast-on edge and with WS facing for next row, shape armhole as follows:

shape armhole

Cont to dec at front edge as set and bind off 3 sts at beg of next row.

Dec 1 st at armhole edge on 3 foll alt rows.

Keeping armhole edge straight, work in patt and cont to dec front slope as set until all decs are complete and armhole measures 9$\frac{1}{2}$ (10$\frac{1}{4}$, 11)" (24 [25, 26])cm, ending with WS facing for next row.

shape shoulder

Bind off 9 (10, 11) sts at beg of next row.

Work 1 row. Bind off rem 9 (10, 11) sts.

to knit the left front:

Work the buttonholes when reached as follows:

Buttonhole row 1 (RS) Rib 5 sts, bind off next 2 sts, rib and patt to end of row as set.

Buttonhole row 2 Work in patt, casting on 2 sts over sts bound off in previous row.

These 2 rows form buttonhole and are positioned on left front when reached as follows:

Work 4 (4, 6) rows, make first buttonhole on next 2 rows, ** work 14 rows, make buttonhole on next 2 rows; rep from ** 3 times more.

Using size 10$\frac{1}{2}$ (7mm) needles, cast on 47 (49, 51) sts and work in rib as follows:

Row 1 (RS) [K2 (1, 1), p1] 1 (1, 2) times, [k2, p1] to last 14 sts, k2, [p1, k1] 6 times.

Row 2 [P1, k1] 6 times, [p2, k1] to last 2 (1, 3) sts, p2 (1, 1), k0 (0, 1), p0 (0, 1).

Rep last 2 rows until work measures 1$\frac{1}{2}$ (1$\frac{1}{2}$, 2)" (4 [4, 5])cm, ending with RS facing for next row and making the first buttonhole as given above.

Change to size 11 (7.5mm) needles and work as follows:

Row 1 (inc row) (RS) K1, p1, k1, [k1, p1] 2 (3, 4) times, k1, Tw2R, p3, [k1, inc in next st] 6 times, k2, p3, Tw2R, p3, [p1, k1] 6 times. **53 (55, 57) sts.**

Row 2 [P1, k1] 6 times, k3, p2, k3, work row 2 of Patt A, k3, p3, [k1, p1] 2 (3, 4) times, p1, k1, p1.

Row 3 [K1, p1] 4 (5, 6) times, Tw2R, p3, work row 3 of Patt A, p3, Tw2R, p3, [p1, k1] 6 times.

Row 4 [P1, k1] 6 times, k3, p2, k3, work row 4 of Patt A, k3, p2, [k1, p1] 4 (5, 6) times.

Row 5 K1, p1, k1, [k1, p1] 2 (3, 4) times, k1, Tw2R, p3, work row 5 of Patt A, p3, Tw2R, p3, [p1, k1] 6 times.

The last 4 rows set the position of the pattern panel and form the twisted sts, 12-st ribbed front band, 5 (7, 9) sts in moss st at side, and 3-st ribbed pocket edging.

Working correct patt panel rows and buttonholes, work even in patt as set until front measures 6" (15.5cm) from cast-on edge, ending with RS facing for next row.

Next row Patt as set, but work first 8 (10, 12) sts in moss stitch.

Work even in patt with buttonholes as now set until front measures 16$\frac{1}{4}$ (16$\frac{3}{4}$, 17$\frac{1}{4}$)" (42 [43, 44])cm from cast-on edge, ending with RS facing for next row.

shape front slope

Next row Patt to last 12 sts, turn and leave these sts on a holder for collar.

Dec 1 st (see notes on fully fashioned shaping, page 80) at neck edge on next row and every foll 3rd row until 24 (26, 28) sts rem, then on every foll alt row until 18 (20, 22) sts rem, **and at the same time,** when work measures 16¾ (17¼, 17¾)" (43 [44, 45])cm from cast-on edge and ending with RS facing for next row, shape armhole as follows:

shape armhole

Cont to dec at front edge as set, bind off 3 sts at beg of next row.

Dec 1 st at armhole edge on 3 foll alt rows.

Keeping armhole edge straight, work in patt and cont to dec front slope as set until all decs are complete and armhole measures 9½ (10¼, 11)" (24 [25, 26])cm, ending with RS facing for next row.

shape shoulder

Bind off 9 (10, 11) sts at beg of next row.

Work 1 row.

Bind off rem 9 (10, 11) sts.

to knit the sleeves:

Using size 10½ (7mm) needles, cast on 38 (42, 46) sts and work 2¼ (2¼, 2¾)" (6 [6, 7])cm in rib as given for Back, ending with RS facing for next row.

Change to size 11 (7.5mm) needles and work as follows:

Row 1 (inc row) (RS) [K1, p1] 3(4,5) times, k1, Tw2R, p3, [k1, inc in next st] 6 times, k2, p3, Tw2R, [k1, p1] 3 (4, 5) times, k1. **44 (48, 52) sts.**

Row 2 [P1, k1] 3 (4, 5) times, p3, k3, work row 2 of Patt A, k3, p3, [k1, p1] 3 (4, 5) times.

The last row sets the position of the moss st, twist sts, and cable panel.

Cont in patt, inc 1 st at each end of next row and every foll 8th row until there are 62 (66, 70) sts, taking all inc sts into moss st.

Work even in patt until sleeve measures 19 (19¾, 20½)" (48 [50, 52])cm from cast-on edge, ending with RS facing for next row.

shape top of sleeve

Bind off 3 sts at beg of next 2 rows. **56 (60, 64) sts.**

Dec 1 st at each end of next row and every foll RS row until 34 (38, 42) sts rem, then dec 1 st at each end of every row until 20 (24, 28) sts rem, ending with WS facing for next row.

Next row (WS) P1 (2, 4), [p2tog, p1] to last 4 (4, 3) sts, [p2tog] 2 (1, 0) times, p0 (2, 3). **13 (17, 21) sts.**
Bind off.

to knit the pocket linings:

(Make 2)

Using size 11 (7.5mm) needles, cast on 18 sts and beg with a k row, work 26 rows in St st, ending with RS facing for next row.
Bind off.

to knit the right front collar:

Sew both shoulder seams.

With WS of work facing and size 11 (7.5mm) needles, rejoin yarn to 12 sts from right front holder and rib one row as set.

Next row (RS) K1, [p1, k1] 5 times, p into front and k into back of last st.

Next row P1, [k1, p1] to end.

Keeping rib correct, inc 1 st at inside neck edge on next and every foll RS row until there are 33 sts.

Work even until collar measures same as neck edge to shoulder seam, ending at straight (outer edge) of collar and placing marker at beg of last row.

Now shape collar in short rows as follows:

Row 1 Rib 3, turn.

Row 2 and every alt row Slip 1, rib to end.

Row 3 Rib 6, turn.

Row 5 Rib 9, turn.

Row 7 Rib 12, turn.

Cont working 3 more sts on every alt row until 3 sts rem unworked, then turn, slip 1, rib to end.

Rib 2 rows across all sts.

Work even until collar reaches center back when slightly stretched, ending at outer edge of collar.

Leave sts on a spare needle.

s/m 44" / 112cm
m/l 46½" / 118cm
xl/xxl 48" / 122cm

s/m 19" / 48cm
m/l 19¾" / 50cm
xl/xxl 20½" / 52cm

s/m 26¼" / 67cm
m/l 27¼" / 70cm
xl/xxl 28¾" / 73cm

to knit the left front collar:

With RS facing and size 11 (7.5mm) needles, rejoin yarn
to 12 sts from left front holder and rib one row as set.
Next row (WS) P1, [k1, p1] 5 times, k into front and
p into back of next st.
Next row K1, [p1, k1] to end.
Complete to match Right Front Collar, reversing shaping
and ending at outer edge of collar.
Holding the needles with right front and left front collar
sts together, bind off the two sets of sts as follows:
Next row * K the 1st st from the front needle tog with
the 1st st from the back needle, p tog the next st from
the back needle with the next st from the front needle,
pass the 1st stitch over the 2nd to bind off; rep from *
to end of row.
Fasten off.

to finish:

Weave in any yarn ends.
Lay pieces out flat, pin if necessary, and gently steam,
but do not flatten cables.
Slipstitch collar in place, matching markers to shoulder
seams.
Sew sleeves into armholes, easing to fit.
Slipstitch row ends of one side edge of pocket linings to
side edge of back, placing cast-on edge on row 1 of
pattern above the rib and bound-off edge matching
markers on row 26.
Sew side seams above and below pocket openings.
Sew sleeve seams.
Slipstitch pocket linings to fronts.
Sew on buttons to match buttonholes.

modern classics

NEW CLASSIC V-NECK AND CREWNECK SWEATERS

A timeless sweater with fully-fashioned detailing and either V-neck or ribbed crewneck—perfect for layering over a white tee or wearing all on its own. Knit it in extra-fine merino yarn or in a light and luxurious cashmere and cotton blend. The slimmer shape and the neckline options make this a new classic design.

sizes:

	s	m	l	xl	xxl	
to fit chest	36	38	40	42	44	inches
	92	97	102	107	112	cm
actual chest	40	$42\frac{1}{2}$	$44\frac{3}{4}$	$47\frac{1}{4}$	$49\frac{1}{4}$	inches
	102	108	114	120	125	cm
actual length	$25\frac{1}{4}$	$26\frac{1}{4}$	$27\frac{1}{2}$	$28\frac{3}{4}$	30	inches
	64	67	70	73	76	cm
sleeve length	19	$19\frac{1}{4}$	$19\frac{3}{4}$	20	$20\frac{1}{2}$	inches
	48	49	50	51	52	cm

materials:

9 (10, 11, 11, 12) balls of Rowan Classic Cashcotton 4-Ply; 35% cotton, 25% polyamide, 18% angora, 13% viscose, 9% cashmere; color mustard; $1\frac{3}{4}$ oz (50g) 197yd (180m), **1** superfine or Rowan Classic Cashsoft 4-Ply; 57% extra fine merino wool, 33% microfiber, 10% cashmere; colour beige; $1\frac{3}{4}$ oz (50g) 197yd (180m), **1** superfine.

Sizes 2 and 3 (2.75mm and 3.25mm) needles

2 stitch holders or safety pins

Tapestry needle

gauge:

28 sts and 36 rows to 4" (10cm) square measured over St st using size 3 (3.25mm) needles. Always work a gauge swatch and change needle size if necessary.

tips and techniques:

Fully fashioned shaping
Decreasing on a knit row:
K3, k2tog, k to last 5 sts, k2tog tbl, k3.
Decreasing on a purl row:
P3, p2tog tbl, p to last 5 sts, p2tog, p3.
Increasing on a knit row:
K3, M1, k to last 3 sts, M1, k3.

both designs

to knit the back:

Using size 2 (2.75mm) needles, cast on 146 (154, 162, 170, 178) sts.
Rib row [k1, p1] to end.
This row forms rib and is repeated.
Work $2\frac{1}{4}$ ($2\frac{1}{4}$, $2\frac{1}{4}$, $2\frac{3}{4}$, $2\frac{3}{4}$)" (6 [6, 6, 7, 7])cm in rib.
Change to size 3 (3.25mm) needles and beg with a RS (k) row, work in St st until back measures $16\frac{1}{2}$ ($17\frac{1}{4}$, 18, 19, $19\frac{3}{4}$)" (42 [44, 46, 48, 50])cm from cast-on edge, ending with RS facing for next row.

shape armholes
Bind off 7 sts at beg of next 2 rows. **132 (140, 148, 156, 164) sts.**
Dec 1 st at each end of next 3 rows [126 (134, 142, 150, 158) sts], then on foll 2 alt rows [122 (130, 138, 144, 152) sts], then on 2 foll 4th rows. **118 (126, 134, 142, 150) sts. ****
Work even until armhole measures $8\frac{3}{4}$ (9, $9\frac{1}{2}$, $9\frac{3}{4}$, $10\frac{1}{4}$)" (22 [23, 24, 25, 26])cm, ending with RS facing for next row.

shape shoulders and back neck
Bind off 11 (12, 13, 14, 15) sts at beg of next 2 rows. **96 (102, 108, 114, 120) sts.**

Next row Bind off 11 (12, 13, 14, 15) sts, work until
14 (15, 16, 17, 18) sts on RH needle, turn and work on
these sts only for first side of neck.
Bind off 4 sts at beg of next row.
Bind off rem 10 (11, 12, 13, 14) sts.
With RS facing, rejoin yarn to rem sts, bind off center
46 (48, 50, 52, 54) sts and k to end.
Complete to match first side, reversing all shaping.

crew-neck sweater

to knit the front:

Work as Back to **. 118 (126, 134, 142, 150) sts.
Work even until front measures 22½ (23½, 24¼, 25½,
26¾)" (57 [60, 62, 65, 68])cm, ending with RS facing for
next row.

shape neck
Next row (RS) K48 (51, 54, 57, 60) sts, turn and work
on these sts only for first side of neck.
Bind off 3 sts at beg of next row. 45 (48, 51, 54,
57) sts.
Dec 1 st at neck edge of next 5 rows, then on foll
8 alt rows. 32 (35, 38, 41, 44) sts.
Work even until armhole matches Back to start of
shoulder shaping, ending with RS facing for next row.

shape shoulder
Bind off 11 (12, 13, 14, 15) sts at beg of next row and
foll alt row.
P 1 row.
Bind off rem 10 (11, 12, 13, 14) sts.
With RS facing, slip center 22 (24, 26, 28, 30) sts onto
holder, rejoin yarn to rem sts and k to end.
Complete to match first side, reversing shaping.

to knit the neckband:

Sew right shoulder seam.
With RS facing and size 2 (2.75mm) needles, pick up
and k 24 (24, 26, 26, 26) sts down left front neck,
k across 22 (24, 26, 28, 30) sts from front neck holder,
pick up and k 24 (24, 26, 26, 26) sts up right front neck,
and 54 (56, 58, 60, 62) sts around shaped back neck
edge. 124 (128, 136, 140, 144) sts.
Work 1¼" (3cm) in k1, p1 rib.
Bind off in rib.

to finish:

Weave in any yarn ends.
Lay work out flat and gently steam each piece.
Sew left shoulder and neckband seam.
Sew sleeves into armholes, easing to fit.
Sew side and sleeve seams, using mattress stitch.

v-neck sweater

to knit the front:

Work as for Back to **. 118 (126, 134, 142, 150) sts.
P 1 row.

shape neck with integral ribbed band
Next row (RS) K48 (52, 56, 60, 64) sts, k2tog tbl, k2,
[p1, k1] 3 times, p1, turn and leave rem 59 (63, 67, 71,
75) sts on a holder.
Work each side of neck separately.
Next row [K1, p1] 3 times, k1, p to end of row.
Keeping 7sts in rib as set for the band, dec 1 st at neck
edge on every 3rd row until 39 (42, 45, 48, 51) sts rem.
Work even until armhole matches Back to shoulder
shaping, ending with RS facing for next row.

shape shoulder
Next row Bind off 11 (12, 13, 14, 15) sts, k to last
7 sts, turn and leave rib sts on a holder.
P 1 row.
Bind off 11 (12, 13, 14, 15) sts at beg of next row.
P 1 row.
Bind off rem 10 (11, 12, 13, 14) sts.
With RS facing, rejoin yarn to rem sts and work as follows:
Next row [P1, k1] 3 times, p1, k2, k2tog, k to end.
Next row P to last 7 sts, [k1, p1] 3 times, k1.
Complete to match first side, reversing all shaping.

to knit the sleeves:

Using size 2 (2.75mm) needles, cast on 60 (64, 68, 72,
76) sts and work 2¼ (2¼, 2¼, 2¾, 2¾)" (6 [6, 6, 7,
7])cm in k1, p1 rib as given for Back.
Change to size 3 (3.25mm) needles and beg with a k
row, work in St st, inc 1 st (see notes on fully fashioned
shaping, page 90) at each end of next row and every foll
6th row until there are 82 (86, 90, 94, 98) sts and then
every foll 8th row until there are 100 (104, 108, 112,
116) sts.

s 40" / 102cm
m 42½" / 108cm
l 44¾" / 114cm
xl 47¼" / 120cm
xxl 49¼" / 125cm

s 19" / 48cm
m 19¼" / 49cm
l 19¾" / 50cm
xl 20" / 51cm
xxl 20½" / 52cm

s 25¼" / 64cm
m 26¼" / 67cm
l 27½" / 70cm
xl 28¾" / 73cm
xxl 30" / 76cm

Work even until sleeve measures 19 (19¼, 19¾, 20, 20½)" (48 [49, 50, 51, 52])cm from cast-on edge, ending with RS facing for next row.

shape top of sleeve

Bind off 7 sts at beg of next 2 rows. **86 (90, 94, 98, 102) sts.**

Dec 1 st (see notes above on fully fashioned shaping) at each end of next 3 rows [80 (84, 88, 92, 96) sts], then on foll 2 alt rows [76 (80, 84, 88, 92) sts], then on 2 foll 4th rows. **72 (76, 80, 84 88) sts.**

Dec 1 st at each end of 15 foll alt rows. **42 (46, 50, 54, 58) sts.**

Dec 1 st at each end of next 5 rows. **32 (36, 40, 44, 45) sts.**

P 1 row.

Bind off 5 sts at beg of next 2 rows. **22 (26, 30, 34, 38) sts.**

K 1 row.

Bind off rem 22 (26, 30, 34, 38) sts.

to make up:

Weave in any yarn ends.

Lay work out flat and gently steam each piece.

Sew shoulder seams.

back neckband

Using size 3 (3.25mm) needles, slip 7 sts from right front holder onto needle, rejoin yarn and work in rib as set until band when slightly stretched, fits across back neck edge to reach 7 sts on left front holder.

Graft 2 sets of 7 sts together.

Sew band to back neck edge.

to finish:

Sew sleeves into armholes, easing to fit.

Sew side and sleeve seams, using mattress stitch.

FINE-KNIT CARDIGAN

A slim-fit cardigan with a deep V-neck, worked in double-knitting-weight, natural bamboo yarn. This garment has a lustrous sheen and excellent drape. With integral button bands and no pockets to get in the way, this cardigan is a modern wardrobe staple with very clean lines.

sizes:

	s	m	l	xl	xxl	
to fit chest	36	38	40	42	44	inches
	92	97	102	107	112	cm
actual chest	41	43	44¾	46½	48	inches
	104	109	114	118	122	cm
actual length	25¼	26¼	27½	28¾	30	inches
	64	67	70	73	76	cm
sleeve length	19	19¼	19¾	20	20½	inches
	48	49	50	51	52	cm

materials:

15 (16, 17, 18, 19) balls of Rowan Classic Bamboo Soft; 100% bamboo; colour purple; 1¾ oz (50g) 112yd (110m), **2** fine.

Sizes 3 and 5 (3.25mm and 3.75mm) needles

5 natural horn buttons, 1" in diameter

gauge:

25 sts and 30 rows to 4" (10cm) square measured over St st using size 5 (3.75mm) needles. Always work a gauge swatch and change needle size if necessary.

tips and techniques:

Take care not to split the bamboo yarn. Knit slowly and enjoy its unique character.

As the button and buttonhole bands are integral, join new balls of yarn at side and armhole edges when working the two fronts.

Fully fashioned shaping

Decreasing on a knit row:
K3, k2tog, k to last 5 sts, k2tog tbl, k3.
Decreasing on a purl row:
P3, p2tog tbl, p to last 5 sts, p2tog, p3.
Increasing on a knit row:
K3, M1, k to last 3 sts, M1, k3.

to knit the back:

Using size 3 (3.25mm) needles, cast on 134 (140, 146, 150, 156) sts.
Rib row [K1, p1] to end of row.
This row forms rib and is repeated.
Work 2¼ (2¼, 2¼, 2¾, 2¾)" (6 [6, 6, 7, 7])cm in rib.
Change to size 5 (3.75mm) needles and beg with a k row, work in St st until back measures 16½ (17¼, 18, 19, 19¾)" (42 [44, 46, 48, 50])cm from cast-on edge, ending with RS facing for next row.

shape armholes

Bind off 6 sts at beg of next 2 rows. **122 (128, 134, 138, 144) sts.**
Dec 1 st (see notes on fully fashioned shaping above) at each end of next 3 rows, then on foll 2 RS rows, then on 2 foll 4th rows. **108 (114, 120, 124, 130) sts.**
Work even until armhole measures 8¾ (9, 9½, 9¾, 10¼)" (22 [23, 24, 25, 26])cm, ending with RS facing for next row.

shape shoulders and back neck

Bind off 10 (11, 12, 12, 13) sts at beg of next 2 rows.
Next row Bind off 11 (12, 12, 13, 13) sts, work until 16 (16, 17, 17, 18) sts on RH needle, turn and work on these sts only for first side of neck.
Bind off 4 sts at beg of next row.
Bind off rem 12 (12, 13, 13, 14) sts.
With RS facing, slip next 34 (36, 38, 40, 42) sts onto a holder, rejoin yarn to rem sts and work to end of row.
Complete to match first side, reversing shaping.

to knit the right front:

Using size 3 (3.25mm) needles, cast on 71 (74, 77, 80, 83) sts and work in rib as follows:

Rib row 1 (RS) [P1, k1] to last 1 (0, 1, 0, 1) st, p1 (0, 1, 0, 1).

Rib row 2 K0 (1, 0, 1, 0), [p1, k1] to end of row.

Rep last 2 rows until work measures 2¼ (2¼, 2¼, 2¾, 2¾)" (6 [6, 6, 7, 7])cm.

Change to size 5 (3.75mm) needles.

Row 1 (RS) [P1, k1] 4 times, p1, k to end of row.

Row 2 P to last 9 sts, [k1, p1] 4 times, k1.

These 2 rows form St st with 9-st ribbed front band. Work in patt as set until front measures 15¾ (16½, 17¼, 18, 18¾)" (40 [42, 44, 46, 48])cm from cast-on edge, ending with RS facing for next row.

shape front slope

Next row [P1, k1] 4 times, p1, k2tog, k to end.

Cont to dec 1 st (inside front ribbed band as before) on every foll 4th row, **and at the same time** when front measures 16½ (17¼, 18, 19, 19¾)" (42 [44, 46, 48, 50])cm, ending with WS facing for next row, shape armhole as follows:

shape armhole

Bind off 6 sts at beg of next row.

Dec 1 st (see note on fully fashioned shaping, page 96) at armhole edge on next 3 rows, then on foll 2 RS rows, then on 2 foll 4th rows.

Keeping armhole straight, cont to dec at front edge only until 42 (44, 46, 47, 49) sts rem.

Work even until armhole measures 8¾ (9, 9½, 9¾, 10¼)" (22 [23, 24, 25, 26])cm, ending with WS facing for next row.

shape shoulder

Bind off 10 (11, 12, 12, 13) sts at beg of next row. Work 1 row.

Next row Bind off 11 (12, 12, 13, 13) sts, p to last 9 sts, turn and leave 9 rib sts on a holder.

Work 1 row.

Bind off rem 12 (12, 13, 13, 14) sts.

to knit the left front:

Using size 3 (3.25mm) needles, cast on 71 (74, 77, 80, 83) sts and work in rib as follows:

Rib row 1 (RS) P1 (0, 1, 0, 1) [k1, p1] to end of row.

Rib row 2 [K1, p1] to last 9 sts, k1 (0, 1, 0, 1).

Rep last 2 rows until work measures 1 (1, 1, 1¼, 1¼)" (2.5 [2.5, 2.5, 3, 3])cm from cast-on edge, ending with WS facing for next row.

Buttonhole row (WS) Rib 4, yo, work 2tog, rib 3, patt to end.

Cont in rib until front measures 2¼ (2¼, 2¼, 2¾, 2¾)" (6 [6, 6, 7, 7])cm, ending with RS facing for next row.

Change to size 5 (3.75mm) needles.

Row 1 (RS) K to last 9 sts, [p1, k1] 4 times, p1.

Row 2 [K1, p1] 4 times, k1, p to end of row.

These 2 rows form St st with 9-st ribbed front band. Rep last 2 rows until work measures 15¾ (16½, 17¼, 18, 18¾)" (40 [42, 44, 46, 48])cm from cast-on edge, making 4 more buttonholes at 3½ (3⅝, 3¾, 3⅞, 4)" (9 [9.25, 9.5, 9.75, 10])cm intervals and ending with RS facing for next row.

shape front slope

Next row (RS) K to last 11 sts, k2tog tbl, p1, [k1, p1] to end of row.

Cont to dec 1 st (inside front ribbed band as before) on every foll 4th row, **and at the same time** when front measures 16½ (17¼, 18, 19, 19¾)" (42 [44, 46, 48, 50])cm and ending with RS facing for next row, shape armhole as follows:

shape armhole

Bind off 6 sts at beg of next row.

Dec 1 st (see note on fully fashioned shaping, page 96) at armhole edge on next 3 rows, then on foll 2 RS rows, then on 2 foll 4th rows.

Keeping armhole straight, cont to dec at front edge only until 42 (44, 46, 47, 49) sts rem.

Work even until armhole measures 8¾ (9, 9½, 9¾, 10¼)" (22 [23, 24, 25, 26])cm, ending with RS facing for next row.

shape shoulder

Bind off 10 (11, 12, 12, 13) sts at beg of next row. Work 1 row.

Next row Bind off 11 (12, 12, 13, 13) sts, k to last 9 sts, turn and leave 9 rib sts on a holder.

Work 1 row. Bind off rem 12 (12, 13, 13, 14) sts.

to knit the sleeves:

Using size 3 (3.25mm) needles, cast on 52 (56, 60, 64, 68) sts and work 2¼" (6cm) in k1, p1 rib as given for Back. Change to size 5 (3.75mm) needles and beg with a k row, work 2 rows in St st.

s 41" / 104cm
m 43" / 109cm
l 44³/₄" / 114cm
xl 46¹/₂" / 118cm
xxl 48" / 122cm

s 19" / 48cm
m 19¹/₄" / 49cm
l 19³/₄" / 50cm
xl 20" / 51cm
xxl 20¹/₂" / 52cm

s 25¹/₄" /64cm
m 26¹/₄" / 67cm
l 27¹/₂" / 70cm
xl 28³/₄" / 73cm
xxl 30" / 76cm

Next row (RS) K3, M1, k to last 3 sts, M1, k3.
Cont in St st, inc 1 st as before on every foll 6th row until there are 92 (96, 100, 104, 108) sts.
Work even until sleeve measures 19 (19¹/₄, 19³/₄, 20, 20¹/₂)" (48 [49, 50, 51, 52])cm from cast-on edge, ending with RS facing for next row.

shape top of sleeve
Bind off 6 sts at beg of next 2 rows. 80 (84, 88, 92, 96) sts.
Dec 1 st at each end of next 3 rows. 74 (78, 82, 86, 90) sts.
Work 1 row.
Dec 1 st at each end of next row and every foll RS row until 52 (56, 60, 64, 68) sts rem, ending with RS facing for next row.
Dec 1 st each end of next 12 rows. 28 (32, 36, 40, 44) sts.
Bind off 5 sts at beg of next 2 rows.
Bind off rem 18 (22, 26, 30, 34) sts.

to make up:
Weave in any yarn ends.
Lay work out flat, pin if necessary, and gently steam under a cloth to protect the yarn; **do not press**.

Graft shoulder seams.

button band
With RS facing and size 5 (3.75mm) needles, rib across 9 sts on right front holder.
Cont in rib until band, when slightly stretched, fits to center back neck, ending with WS facing for next row.
Bind off in rib.

buttonhole band
With RS facing and size 5 (3.75mm) needles, rib across 9 sts on left front holder.
Cont in rib until band, when slightly stretched, fits to center back neck, ending with RS facing for next row.
Bind off in rib.

to finish:
WSew sleeves into armholes, easing to fit.
Sew side and sleeve seams from armhole to cuff edge and hem, matching ribs and using mattress stitch.
Graft neckband seams and slipstitch band to back neck edge. Sew on buttons.

PLAIN, ARGYLE, & CHECKERED VESTS

The vest is a perennial piece, great in a plain color or easily customized with a graphic pattern. This simple design is knitted in a beautiful cotton and cashmere blend in a melange or tonal mixture yarn, to give subtle texture and a good base for the bolder colors of the argyle or check version.

sizes:

	s	m	l	xl	xxl	
to fit chest	36	38	40	42	44	inches
	92	97	102	107	112	cm
actual chest	36	39	41¼	43¼	46	inches
	92	99	105	110	117	cm
actual length	24½	25¼	26	26¾	27½	inches
	62	64	66	68	70	cm

materials:

for the plain vest

6 (6, 7, 7, 8) balls of Rowan Classic Cashcotton 4-Ply; 35% cotton, 25% polyamide, 18% angora, 13% viscose, 9% cashmere; color lilac; 1¾ oz (50g) 197yd (180m); **1** superfine.

Sizes 2 and 3 (2.75mm and 3.25mm) needles

Tapestry needle

for the argyle vest

6 (6, 7, 8, 9) balls of Rowan Classic Cashcotton 4-Ply; 35% cotton, 25% polyamide, 18% angora, 13% viscose, 9% cashmere; 1¾ oz (50g) 197yd (180m); **1** superfine in cork (A) and 1 ball in each of jet (B), treacle (C), light aubergine (D), thunder (E), and sea foam (F)

Sizes 2 and 3 (2.75mm and 3.25mm) needles

Tapestry needle

for the checkered vest

6 (6, 7, 7, 8) balls of Rowan Classic Cashcotton 4-Ply; 35% cotton, 25% polyamide, 18% angora, 13% viscose, 9% cashmere; 1¾ oz (50g) 197yd (180m), **1** superfine in sea foam (A) and 1 ball in treacle (B).

Sizes 2 and 3 (2.75mm and 3.25mm) needles

Size C-2 (2.75mm) crochet hook

Tapestry needle

gauge:

28 sts and 36 rows to 4" (10cm) square measured over St st using size 3 (3.25mm) needles. Always work a gauge swatch and change needle size if necessary.

tips and techniques:

Fully fashioned shaping
Decreasing on a knit row:
K3, k2tog, k to last 5 sts, k2tog tbl, k3.
Decreasing on a purl row:
P3, p2tog tbl, p to last 5 sts, p2tog, p3.
Increasing on a knit row:
K3, M1, k to last 3 sts, M1, k3.

plain vest

to knit the back:

Using size 2 (2.75mm) needles, cast on 130 (140, 148, 156, 166) sts.

Rib row [K1, p1] to end of row.

This row forms rib and is repeated.

Work 2" (5cm) in rib, inc 1 st on last row. 131 (141, 149, 157, 167) sts. **

Change to size 3 (3.25mm) needles and beg with a k row, work 126 (130, 134, 136, 140) rows in St st, ending with RS facing for next row.

shape armholes

Bind off 8 (8, 9, 9, 9) sts at beg of next 2 rows. 115 (125, 131, 139, 149) sts.

Dec 1 st (see notes on fully fashioned shaping, page 96) at each end of next 5 rows. 105 (115, 121, 129, 139) sts.

Then dec 1 st at each end of foll 3 (4, 4, 5, 6) RS rows. 99 (107, 113, 119, 127) sts. ***

Work even in St st for 67 (67, 71, 73, 75) rows more, ending with RS facing for next row.

shape shoulders and back neck

Bind off 9 (10, 10, 11, 12) sts at beg of next 2 rows. 81 (87, 93, 97, 103) sts.

Next row (RS) Bind off 9 (10, 11, 11, 12) sts, work until there are 12 (13, 14, 15, 16) sts on RH needle, turn and leave rem sts on a holder.

Work each side separately.

Bind off 4 sts at beg of next row.

Bind off rem 8 (9, 10, 11, 12) sts.

With RS facing, rejoin yarn to rem sts, slip center 39 (41, 43, 45, 47) sts onto a holder and work to end of row.

Complete to match first side, reversing shaping.

to knit the front:

Work as given for Back to ***. 99 (107, 113, 119, 127) sts.

Work even for 7 (7, 7, 7, 5) rows more, so ending with RS facing for next row.

divide for neck

Next row K49 (53, 56, 59, 63) sts, turn and leave rem sts on a holder.

Work each side of neck separately.

P 1 row.

Next row K to last 5 sts, k2tog tbl, k3.

Next row P.

Rep last 2 rows until 26 (29, 31, 33, 36) sts rem, ending with RS facing for next row.

Work even for 12 (10, 12, 12, 14) rows more, ending with RS facing for next row.

shape shoulder

Bind off 9 (10, 10, 11, 12) sts at beg of next row and 9 (10, 11, 11, 12) sts on foll RS row.

Work 1 row.

Bind off rem 8 (9, 10, 11, 12) sts.

With RS facing, slip center st onto a holder, rejoin yarn to rem sts and k to end of row.

P 1 row.

Next row K3, k2tog, k to end.

Next row P.

s 36" / 92cm
m 39" / 99cm
l 41¼" / 105cm
xl 43¼" / 110cm
xxl 46" / 117cm

s 24½" / 62cm
m 25¼" / 64cm
l 26" / 66cm
xl 26¾" / 68cm
xxl 27½" / 70cm

Rep last 2 rows until 26 (29, 31, 33, 36) sts rem, ending with RS facing for next row.

Work even for 13 (11, 13, 13, 15) rows more, ending with WS facing for next row.

Bind off 9 (10, 10, 11, 12) sts at beg of next row and 9 (10, 11, 11, 12) sts on foll WS row.

Work 1 row.

Bind off rem 8 (9, 10, 11, 12) sts.

to knit the neckband:

Sew right shoulder seam.

With RS facing and size 2 (2.75mm) needles, pick up and k 47 (49, 51, 53, 55) sts down left front neck, k 1 st from holder (place a marker on this stitch), pick up and k 47 (49, 51, 53, 55) sts up right front neck, 4 sts down right back neck, then k across 39 (41, 43, 45, 47) sts on back neck holder, then pick up and k 4 sts up left back neck. **142 (148, 154, 160, 166) sts.**

Row 1 (WS) [P1, k1] to end of row.

Row 2 (RS) Rib to within 2 sts of marked st, k2tog tbl, k marked stitch, k2tog, rib to end.

Row 3 Rib to marked st, p1, rib to end.

Rep last 2 rows until neckband measures 1" (2.5cm).

Bind off in rib.

to knit the armbands:

Sew left shoulder seam and neckband seam.

With RS facing and size 2 (2.75mm) needles, pick up and k 132 (138, 144, 150, 156) sts evenly around armholes and work 1" (2.5cm) in k1, p1 rib as given for Back.

Bind off in rib.

to finish:

Weave in any yarn ends.

Lay work out flat and gently steam.

Sew side seams, using mattress stitch.

argyle vest

chart note

The 19-st chart panel consists of a single diamond worked over repeats of 36 rows. Work the diamonds on the front of the vest using the Intarsia method—using a separate ball of yarn for each color area and twisting yarns at color change to avoid holes. Duplicate stitch the raker crossing lines on the completed front.

Each garment size starts on a different RS (k) chart row so that the V-neck shaping begins above a whole diamond. Read all RS (k) chart rows from right to left and WS (p) rows from left to right.

Each vertical line of diamonds is worked in a different color with a contrast color raker. Apart from the diamonds and rakers, the front is worked using yarn A.

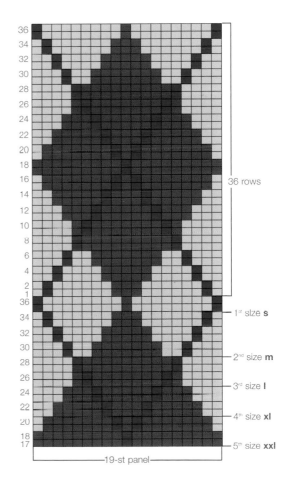

to knit the back, neckband, and armbands:

Using A, work as given for Plain Vest.

to knit the front:

Using A, work as given for Back of Plain Vest to **. Change to size 3 (3.25mm) needles and work in St st in chart patt, beg with a RS (k) row on the row indicated on chart for your chosen size and placing 19-st panels on first row as follows:

Row 1 (RS) K16 (21, 25, 29, 34) in A, k correct row of chart using B for diamond and A for background, k21 in A, k correct row of chart using C for diamond and A for background, k21 in A, k correct row of chart using D for diamond and A for background, k16 (21, 25, 29, 34) in A.

Cont in St st chart patt as set, **and at the same time** complete as given for Front of Plain Vest for all shaping.

to finish:

Duplicate stitch the raker crossing lines (see above right), working E on B diamonds, D on C diamonds, and F on D diamonds.
Finish as given for Plain Vest.

to duplicate stitch:

1 Thread a tapestry needle with yarn the same weight as the stitch you are working over. Bring the needle out at the base of the first stitch you want to cover, then take it under the base of the stitch above.
2 Take the needle back through the base of the first stitch and out at the base of the next stitch. Continue to cover each stitch in this way.

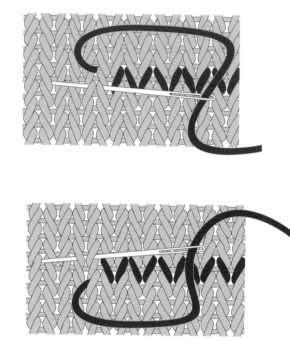

checkered vest

to knit the back:

Using A, work as given for Plain Vest.

to knit the front:

Using A, work as given for Back of Plain Vest to **.
Change to size 3 (3.25mm) needles and beg with a
k row, work in St st as follows: 18 rows in A, 1 row
in B (a k row), 18 rows in A, 1 row in B (a p row).
These 38 rows form the patt and are repeated.
Cont in patt as set, **and at the same time** complete as
given for Front of Plain Vest for all shaping.

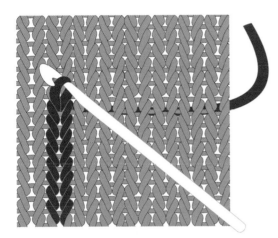

to create the check effect:

Mark the positions of the vertical lines of chain stitch on
completed Front in first row just above rib as follows:
With RS facing and counting from the right, mark
position of a vertical line in 10th (15th, 19th, 9th, 14th) st,
then in every foll 14th st across Front, so ending with a
line in 10th (15th, 19th, 9th, 14th) st from the left side
edge.
Using size C-2 (2.75mm) crochet hook and B, work
each vertical line of chain stitch starting at marked
positions on Front as follows:
With yarn at back, insert the crochet hook through first
st from front to back and draw through a loop, insert

hook into st one or two rows directly above the original
point (depending on length of stitch required) and draw
through another loop, then draw this through the loop
on the hook to make a chain stitch on the right side of
the fabric. Continue in this way all the way up Front to
create check patt. To fasten off, cut the yarn and draw
through the last st.

to knit the neckband and armbands:

Using A, work as given for Plain Vest, but work last row
of rib and bind-off row using B.

to finish:

Work as given for Plain Vest.

FUNNEL-NECK SWEATER

A beautiful fitted yet casual sweater, with oversized rib stitch yoke, integrated rib stitch elbow patch detail, and a simple funnel neck. It is knit in thick but oh-so soft merino wool and kid mohair yarn for rugged comfort—sure to become one of those "old friend" favorite pieces.

sizes:

	s	m	l	xl	xxl	
to fit chest	36	38	40	42	44	inches
	92	97	102	107	112	cm
actual chest	42	44	46½	48¾	51¼	inches
	107	112	118	124	130	cm
actual length	27½	27½	28¼	28¼	29	inches
	70	70	72	72	74	cm
sleeve length	19	19¼	19¾	20	20½	inches
	48	49	50	51	52	cm

materials:

10 (10, 11, 11, 12) balls of Rowan Cocoon; 80% merino wool, 20% kid mohair; color charcoal; 3½ oz (100g) 126yd (115m); **5** bulky.

Sizes 10 and 10½ (6.5mm and 7mm) needles

gauge:

14 sts and 16 rows to 4" (10cm) square measured over St st using size 10½ (7mm) needles. Always work a gauge swatch and change needle size if necessary.

tips and techniques:

Fully fashioned shaping
Work fully fashioned shaping as given on page 114.

to knit the back:

Using size 10 (6.5mm) needles, cast on 76 (80, 84, 88, 92) sts.
Rib row [K1, p1] to end of row.

Rep last row until work measures 3¼" (8cm), inc 1 st at center of last row. **77 (81, 85, 89, 93) sts.**
Change to size 10½ (7mm) needles and beg with a k row, work in St st until back measures 18½ (18, 18½, 18, 18½)" (47 [46, 47, 46, 47])cm from cast-on edge, ending with RS facing for next row.

shape armholes
Bind off 4 sts at beg of next 2 rows. **69 (73, 77, 81, 85) sts.**

Dec 1 st (see notes on fully fashioned shaping, page 114) at each end of next row and foll 2 RS rows. **63 (67, 71, 75, 79) sts.**

Work even until armhole measures 9 (9½, 9¾, 10¼, 10½)" (23 [24, 25, 26, 27])cm, ending with RS facing for next row.

shape shoulders
Bind off 7 (7, 8, 9, 10) sts at beg of next 2 rows. **49 (53, 55, 57, 59) sts.**

Bind off 7 (8, 9, 10, 10) sts at beg of next 2 rows. **35 (37, 37, 37, 39) sts.**

Change to size 10 (6.5mm) needles and work collar as follows:
Row 1 (RS): P1 (2, 2, 2, 3), [k3, p2] to last 4 (5, 5, 5, 6) sts, k3, p1 (2, 2, 2, 3).
Row 2 K1 (2, 2, 2, 3), [p3, k2] to last 4 (5, 5, 5, 6) sts, p3, k1 (2, 2, 2, 3).
Rep last 2 rows until collar measures 2¾" (7cm), ending with RS facing for next row. Bind off in rib as set.

to knit the front:

Work as given for Back until front measures 16¼ (15¾, 16¼, 15¾, 16¼)" (41 [40, 41, 40, 41])cm from cast-on edge, ending with RS facing for next row and placing marker on center stitch of last row.

Start working the front ribbed yoke on next row as follows, **and at the same time** when work measures 18½ (18, 18½, 18, 18½)" (47 [46, 47, 46, 47])cm from cast-on edge and with RS facing, shape armholes as

given for Back:

Row 1 (RS) K to 3 sts before marked st, p2, k3, p2, k to end of row.

Rows 2 and 3 K and p sts as set.

Row 4 (WS) P to 8 sts before marked st, [k2, p3] 3 times, k2, p to end of row.

Rows 5 and 6 K and p sts as set.

Row 7 (RS) K to 13 sts before marked st, [p2, k3} 5 times, p2, k to end of row.

Rows 8 and 9 K and p sts as set.

Row 10 (WS) P to 18 sts before marked st, [k2, p3] 7 times; k2, p to end of row.

Rows 11 and 12 K and p sts as set.

Cont in this way, working 5 more sts into rib at each side of center marked st on next row and every foll 3rd row until all sts are being worked in rib.

Work even in rib until armhole measures 9 (9½, 9¾, 10¼, 10½)" (23 [24, 25, 26, 27])cm, ending with RS facing for next row.

shape shoulders

Bind off 7 (7, 8, 9, 10) sts at beg of next 2 rows. 49 (53, 55, 57, 59) sts.

Bind off 7 (8, 9, 10, 10) sts at beg of next 2 rows. 35 (37, 37, 37, 39) sts.

Change to size 10 (6.5mm) needles and cont in rib as set until collar measures 2¾" (7cm), ending with RS facing for next row. Bind off in rib.

to knit the sleeves:

Using size 10 (6.5mm) needles, cast on 34 (34, 36, 36, 38) sts.

Work 3¼" (8cm) in k1, p1 rib as given for Back, inc 1 st at center of last row. 35 (35, 37, 37, 39) sts.

Change to size 10½ (7mm) needles and beg with a k row, work in St st, inc 1 st at each end of 3rd and every foll 4th row, **and at the same time** when work measures 7½ (7¾, 7¾, 8¼, 8¼)" (19 [20, 20, 21, 21])cm from cast-on edge, place a marker on center st and with RS facing, start working ribbed elbow section as follows:

Row 1 (RS) K to 3 sts before marked st, p2, k3, p2, k to end of row.

Row 2 and every foll WS row K and p sts as set.

Row 3 K to 8 sts before marked st, [p2, k3] 3 times, p2, k to end of row.

Row 5 K to 13 sts before marked st, [p2, k3] 5 times, p2, k to end of row.

Row 7 K to 18 sts before marked st, [p2, k3] 7 times, p2, k to end of row.

Rows 9, 11, 13, and 15 K to 23 sts before marked st, [p2, k3] 9 times, p2, k to end of row.

Row 17, 19, 21, and 23 Rep rows 7, 5, 3, and 1.

Row 24 K and p sts as set.

Beg with a k row, work in St st and cont to inc as set until there are 67 (69, 69, 71, 71) sts.

Work even until sleeve measures 19 (19¼, 19¾, 20, 20½)" (48 [49, 50, 51, 52])cm from cast-on edge, ending with RS facing for next row.

shape top of sleeve

Bind off 4 sts at beg of next 2 rows. 59 (61, 61, 63, 63) sts.
Dec 1 st at each end of next row and foll 2 RS rows, then at each end of next 7 rows. 39 (41, 41, 43, 43) sts.
Bind off 13 sts at beg of next 2 rows.
Bind off rem 13 (15, 15, 17, 17) sts.

to finish:

Weave in any yarn ends. Gently steam each piece, without pressing. Graft shoulder seams, and sew collar seams. Sew sleeves into armholes, easing to fit. Sew sleeve and side seams, using mattress stitch.

s 19" / 48cm
m 19¼" / 49cm
l 19¾" / 50cm
xl 20" / 51cm
xxl 20½" / 52cm

s 42" / 107cm
m 44" / 112cm
l 46½" / 118cm
xl 48¾" / 124cm
xxl 51¼" / 130cm

s 27½" / 70cm
m 27½" / 70cm
l 28¼" / 72cm
xl 28¼" / 72cm
xxl 29" / 74cm

CABLED SWEATER

A casual sweater made in rustic Donegal tweed wool yarn, which has the soft natural feel of homespun yarn and characteristic flecks of color. Knit in stockinette stitch with traditional plait stitch panels, this sweater will be naturally moisture-resistant and very durable.

sizes:

	s	m	l	xl	xxl	
to fit chest	36	38	40	42	44	inches
	92	97	102	107	112	cm
actual chest	41¼	43¾	46½	49¼	51½	inches
	105	111	118	125	131	cm
actual length	26½	27	27½	27¾	28¾	inches
	67	69	70	71	73	cm
sleeve length	19	19¼	19¾	20	20½	inches
	48	49	50	51	52	cm

materials:

9 (9, 10, 10, 11) balls of Debbie Bliss Donegal Chunky Tweed; 100% wool; color charcoal; 3½oz (100g) 109yd (100m), (5) bulky.

Sizes 10 and 10½ (6.5mm and 7mm) needles

Cable needle

gauge:

12 sts and 18 rows to 4" (10cm) square measured over St st using size 10½ (7mm) needles. Always work a gauge swatch and change needle size if necessary.

special abbreviations:

C6F slip next 3 sts onto cable needle and hold at front of work, k3 from LH needle, then k3 from cable needle.
C6B slip next 3 sts onto cable needle and hold at back of work, k3 from LH needle, then k3 from cable needle.

tips and techniques:

Fully fashioned shaping
Decreasing on a knit row:
K2, k2tog, k to last 4 sts, k2tog tbl, k2.
Decreasing on a purl row:
P2, p2tog tbl, p to last 4 sts, p2tog, p2.
Increasing on a knit row:
K2, M1, k to last 2 sts, M1, k2.

to knit the back:

Using size 10 (6.5mm) needles, cast on 65 (69, 73, 77, 81) sts.
Row 1 K1, [p1, k1] to end of row.
Row 2 P1, [k1, p1] to end of row.
These 2 rows form rib.
Work 11 (11, 11, 13, 13) rows more in rib.
Change to size 10½ (7mm) needles.
Next row (WS) P12 (13, 14, 15, 16), k3, [p1, inc in next st] 3 times, k3, p17 (19, 21, 23, 25), k3, [p1, inc in next st] 3 times, k3, p12 (13, 14, 15, 16). 71 (75, 79, 83, 87) sts.
Now work in cable patt as follows,
Row 1 (RS) K12 (13, 14, 15, 16), p3, k9, p3, k17 (19, 21, 23, 25), p3, k9, p3, k12 (13, 14, 15, 16).
Row 2 P12 (13, 14, 15, 16), k3, p9, k3, p17 (19, 21, 23, 25), k3, p9, k3, p12 (13, 14, 15, 16).
Rows 3 and 4 Rep rows 1 and 2.
Row 5 K12 (13, 14, 15, 16), p3, k3, C6F, p3, k17 (19, 21, 23, 25), p3, k3, C6F, p3, k12 (13, 14, 15, 16).
Rows 6–8 Rep rows 2, 3, and 4.
Row 9 K12 (13, 14, 15, 16), p3, C6B, k3, p3, k17 (19, 21, 23, 25), p3, C6B, k3, p3, k12 (13, 14, 15, 16).
Row 10 Rep row 2.
Rows 3–10 form the cable patt and are repeated until back measures 17¾ (18, 18, 18, 18½)" (45 [46, 46, 46,

47])cm, ending with RS facing for next row.

shape armholes

Bind off 4 sts at beg of next 2 rows.

Bind off 2 sts at beg of foll 2 rows. 59 (63, 67, 71, 75) sts.

Dec 1 st at each end of next row and foll alt row. 55 (59, 63, 67, 71) sts. **

Work even until armhole measures 8¾ (9, 9½, 9¾, 10¼)" (22 [23, 24, 25, 26])cm, ending with WS facing for next row.

Next row P4 (5, 6, 7, 8), * k3, [p1, p2tog] 3 times, k3, p17 (19, 21, 23, 25), k3, [p1, p2tog] 3 times, k3, p4 (5, 6, 7, 8). 49 (53, 57, 61, 65) sts.

shape back neck and shoulders

Next row (RS) Bind off 7 (8, 9, 10, 11) sts, k until there are 11 (12, 12, 13, 14) sts on RH needle, turn and work on these sts only for first side of neck and shoulder.

Next row Bind off 3 sts, p to end of row.

Bind off rem 8 (9, 9, 10, 11) sts.

With RS facing, slip center 13 (13, 15, 15, 15) sts onto a holder, rejoin yarn to rem sts and patt to end of row.

Complete to match first side, reversing shaping.

to knit the front:

Work as given for Back to **.

Work even until 16 rows less than Back have been worked to shoulders, so ending with RS facing for next row.

shape neck

Next row Patt 22 (24, 26, 28, 30) sts, turn and leave rem sts on a holder.

Bind off 2 (2, 3, 3, 3) sts at beg of next row.

Dec 1 st at neck edge on next row and foll alt row. 18 (20, 21, 23, 25) sts.

Work even for 10 rows.

Next row (WS) P0 (0, 0, 1, 2), k2 (3, 3, 3, 3), [p1, p2tog] 3 times, k3, p4 (5, 6, 7, 8). 15 (17, 18, 20, 22) sts.

shape shoulder

Bind off 7 (8, 9, 10, 11) sts at beg of next row.

Work 1 row.

Bind off rem 8 (9, 9, 10, 11) sts.

With RS facing, slip center 11 sts onto a holder, rejoin yarn to rem 22 (24, 26, 28, 30) sts and patt to end of row.

Complete to match first side, reversing shaping.

to knit the sleeves:

With size 10 (6.5mm) needles, cast on 34 (36, 38, 40, 42) sts and work in rib as follows:

Rib row [K1, p1] to end of row.

This row forms rib.

Work 12 (12, 12, 14, 14) rows more in rib.

Change to size 10½ (7mm) needles.

Next row (WS): P11 (12, 13, 14, 15), k3, [p1, inc in next st] 3 times, k3, p11 (12, 13, 14, 15). 37 (39, 41, 43, 45) sts.

Now work in cable patt as follows:

Row 1 K11 (12, 13, 14, 15), p3, k9, p3, k to end.

Row 2 P11 (12, 13, 14, 15), k3, p9, k3, p to end.

These 2 rows set the position of the central cable outlined with 3 sts in reverse St st and St st at each side. Cont in patt as now set, working cable as given for Back and inc 1 st (see notes on fully fashioned shaping, page 114) at each end of 9th and every foll 6th row until there are 55 (57, 59, 61, 63) sts, taking all inc sts into St st.

Work even until sleeve measures 19 (19¼, 19¾, 20, 20½)" (48 [49, 50, 51, 52])cm from cast-on edge, ending with RS facing for next row.

shape top of sleeve

Bind off 4 sts at beg of next 2 rows.

Bind off 2 sts at beg of next 2 rows. 43 (45, 47, 49, 51) sts.

Dec 1 st at each end of next row and every foll alt row until 13 sts rem, ending with WS facing for next row.

Next row K2, [p1, p2tog] 3 times, k2.

Bind off rem 10 sts.

to knit the neckband:

Sew right shoulder seam.

With RS facing and size 10 (6.5mm) needles, pick up and k 70 (74, 78, 82, 82) sts evenly around neck edge, including 11 sts on center front holder and 13 (13, 15, 15, 15) sts on center back holder.

Work 2¼" (6cm) in k1, p1 rib as given for Sleeves.

Bind off in rib.

s 41¼" / 105cm
m 43¾" / 111cm
l 46½" / 118cm
xl 49¼" / 125cm
xxl 51½" / 131cm

s 19" / 48cm
m 19¼" / 49cm
l 19¾" / 50cm
l 20" / 51cm
xl 20½" / 52cm

s 26½" / 67cm
m 27" / 69cm
l 27½" / 70cm
xl 27¾" / 71cm
xxl 28¾" / 73cm

to finish:

Weave in any yarn ends.

Lay work out flat, pin if necessary, and gently steam, but **do not press** cables or ribs.

Graft left shoulder, and sew neckband seam.

Sew sleeves into armholes, easing to fit and gently stretching around top of sleeve to avoid a "gather."

Sew side and sleeve seams from armhole to cuff edge and hem, using mattress stitch.

accessories

WEEKEND HAT

Knit in stockinette stitch, with a rib trim and a shaped crown, this hat is worked with just one ball of bulky-weight yarn. A very quick knit, it can literally be made in a single evening. The hat is shown here in both basic black and a classic stone shade, but you could make it in a variety of seasonal colors.

size:

one size to fit average adult head

materials:

1 ball of Debbie Bliss Cashmerino Superchunky; 55% merino wool, 33% microfiber, 12% cashmere; colour black or stone; 3½oz (100g) 82yd (75m), **⑤** bulky or Rowan Cocoon, 80% merino wool, 20% kid mohair; color black or stone; 3½oz (100g) 126yd (115m), **⑤** bulky.

Sizes 10 and 10½ (6.5mm and 7mm) needles

Tapestry needle

gauge:

12 sts and 16 rows to 4" (10cm) square measured over St st using size 10½ (7mm) needles. Always work a gauge swatch and change needle size if necessary.

to knit the hat:

Using size 10 (6.5mm) needles, cast on 62 sts and work in rib as follows:
Row 1 (RS) [K2, p1] to last 2 sts, k2.
Row 2 [P2, k1] to last 2 sts, p2.
Rep last 2 rows 3 times more.
Change to size 10½ (7mm) needles and beg with a k row, work 16 rows in St st, dec 1 st on last row.

shape crown

Row 1 (RS) [K4, k2tog] 10 times, k1. **51 sts.**
Work even for 3 rows.
Row 5 [K3, k2tog] 10 times, k1. **41 sts.**
Row 6 P.
Row 7 [K2, k2tog] 10 times, k1. **31 sts.**
Row 8 P.
Row 9 [K1, k2tog] 10 times, k1. **21 sts.**
Row 11 P1, [p2tog] 10 times. **11 sts.**
Cut yarn leaving a long end, thread through rem sts, pull up, and fasten off securely.

to finish:

Weave in any yarn ends.
Lay work out and gently steam.
Sew back seam.

BEANIE

Another basic hat design to make either in a plain color or in a variegated stripe pattern using two complementary shades. Like the hat on pages 122–125, this hat is knitted in stockinette stitch with a shaped crown, but rather than a ribbed band, it has a soft rolled edge.

size:

one size to fit average adult head

materials:

For striped version: 1 ball of Debbie Bliss Cashmerino Aran; 55% merino wool, 33% microfiber, 12% cashmere; color black (A) and stone (B) or burgundy (A) and stone (B); 1¾ oz (50g) 98yd (90m), **4** medium in each of A and B.
For plain version: 2 balls in one color.

Size 7 (4.5mm) needles

Tapestry needle

gauge:

19 sts and 25 rows to 4" (10cm) square measured over St st using size 7 (4.5mm) needles. Always work a gauge swatch and change needle size if necessary.

stripe sequence:

13 rows A.
1 row B.
7 rows A.
3 rows B.
5 rows A.
5 rows B.
3 rows A.
10 rows B.
2 rows A.
12 rows B.

to knit the hat:

For plain version, work entire hat as for striped version but using one color only; and for striped version, cast on with A and work in stripe sequence as follows:
Using A, cast on 86 sts and beg with a k row, work 44 rows in striped St st following stripe sequence, so ending with RS facing for next row.

shape crown

Keeping stripe pattern correct, work as follows:
Row 1 (RS) K9, [k2tog tbl, k1, k2tog, k16] 3 times, k2tog tbl, k1, k2tog, k9. **78 sts.**
Row 2 and all WS rows P.
Row 3 K8, [k2tog tbl, k1, k2tog, k14] 3 times, k2tog tbl, k1, k2tog, k8. **70 sts.**
Row 5 K7, [k2tog tbl, k1, k2tog, k12] 3 times, k2tog tbl, k1, k2tog, k7. **62 sts.**
Row 7 K6, [k2tog tbl, k1, k2tog, k10] 3 times, k2tog tbl, k1, k2tog, k6. **54 sts.**
Row 9 K5, [k2tog tbl, k1, k2tog, k8] 3 times, k2tog tbl, k1, k2tog, k5. **46 sts.**
Row 11 K4, [k2tog tbl, k1, k2tog, k6] 3 times, k2tog tbl, k1, k2tog, k4. **38 sts.**
Row 13 K3, [k2tog tbl, k1, k2tog, k4] 3 times, k2tog tbl, k1, k2tog, k3. **30 sts.**
Row 15 K2, [k2tog tbl, k1, k2tog, k2] 3 times, k2tog tbl, k1, k2tog, k2. **22 sts.**
Row 17 K1, [k2tog tbl, k1, k2tog] 4 times, k1. **14 sts.**
Cut yarn leaving a long end, thread through rem sts, pull up, and fasten off securely.

to finish:

Weave in any yarn ends.
Lay work out and gently and steam.
Sew back seam.

STRIPED SCARF
The simplest of scarves in the softest of yarns.

Worked in garter stitch, this wool scarf is comprised of bands of luxurious baby alpaca yarn. Each stripe is worked in long rows, from end to end, on a circular needle, so the edges of the scarf lie flat and do not curl.

size:

one size approx 7½" (18cm) wide by 43¼" (110cm) long

materials:

3 balls of Rowan Classic Baby Alpaca DK; 100% baby alpaca; 1¾ oz (50g) 109yd (100m); light in each of dark gray (A), light gray (B), and blue-green (C)

Size 6 (4mm) circular needle

One size 7 (4.5mm) needle

gauge:

20 sts and 42 rows to 4" (10cm) square measured over garter st using size 6 (4mm) needles. Always work a gauge swatch and change needle size if necessary.

tips and techniques:

Weave in any yarn ends carefully along the rows of knitting. Do not weave in yarn ends up the side, as this will create a bumpy uneven edge on the scarf.

to knit the scarf:

Using size 6 (4mm) circular needle and A, cast on 220
sts and work 1¼" (3cm) in garter st (k every row).
Change to B and cont in garter st until work
measures 2½" (6cm) from cast-on edge.
Change to C and cont in garter st until work
measures 3¾" (9cm) from cast-on edge.
Change to A and cont in garter st until work
measures 5" (12cm) from cast-on edge.
Change to B and cont in garter st until work
measures 6¼" (15cm) from cast-on edge.
Change to C and cont in garter st until work
measures 7½" (18cm) from cast-on edge.
Bind off firmly, using a size 7 (4.5mm) needle.

to finish:

Weave in any yarn ends.
Lay work out flat and gently steam.

BIG CABLE SCARF

This deceptively simple scarf is worked in super-bulky yarn on big needles to produce an oversized cable design, adding a modern twist to a traditional Aran knitwear motif. The scarf shown here is over 2 yards long, but you could always knit fewer or more cables to adjust the garment to your preferred length.

size:

one size approx 9" (23cm) wide by 92½" (235cm) long

materials:

5 balls of Rowan Big Wool; 100% merino wool; color lime green; 3½oz (100g) 87yd (80m); **(6)** superbulky.

Size 17 (12mm) needles

Cable needle

gauge:

9 sts and 12 rows to 4" (10cm) square measured over St st using size 17 (12mm) needles. Always work a gauge swatch and change needle size if necessary.

special abbreviations:

C12B slip next 6 sts onto cable needle and hold at back of work, k6 from LH needle, then k6 from cable needle.

C12F slip next 6 sts onto cable needle and hold at front of work, k6 from LH needle, then k6 from cable needle.

tips and techniques:

Weave in any yarn ends carefully along the rows of knitting. Do not weave in yarn ends up the side, as this will create a bumpy uneven edge on the scarf.
If desired, use a size larger needle to bind off firmly.

to knit the scarf:

Cast on 26 sts and work in patt as follows:

Row 1 (RS) P4, k18, p4.

Row 2 and all WS rows P.

Row 3 P4, k6, C12F, p4.

Rows 5–10 [Rep rows 1 and 2] 3 times.

Row 11 P4, C12B, k6, p4.

Rows 13–16 [Rep rows 1 and 2] twice.

Rep these 16 rows until knitting measures approx
92½" (235cm), ending with row 16 of patt.

Bind off.

to finish:

Weave in any yarn ends.

Lay work out flat and gently steam, but do not flatten
cable.

RECOMMENDED YARNS

The following is a list of the yarns used for the projects in this book. The yarn characteristics given will be helpful if you are trying to find an alternative yarn. Although I have recommended specific yarns for the projects in the book, you can use substitutes if you like.

If you decide to use an alternative yarn, purchase a substitute yarn that is as close as possible to the original in thickness, weight, and texture so that it will work with the pattern instructions. Buy only one ball to start with, so you can test the effect. Calculate the number of balls you will need by yardage rather than by weight. The recommended knitting-needle size and knitting gauge on the yarn labels are extra guides to the yarn thickness.

To obtain Blue Sky Alpacas, Debbie Bliss, Lanaknits, and Rowan yarns, use the contact information below to find a mail-order supplier or store in your area:

Blue Sky Alpacas
PO Box 88
Cedar, MN 55011
tel: 763-753-5815
email: info@blueskyalpacas.com
www.blueskyalpacas.com

Debbie Bliss
Knitting Fever Inc.
315 Bayview Avenue
Amityville, NY 11701
tel: 516-546-3600
www.knittingfever.com

Lana Knits
Lana Knits Designs Hemp for Knitting
Suite 3B
320 Vernon Street
Nelson, BC V1L 4E4
tel: 888-301-0011
email: info@lanaknits.com
www.lanaknits.com

Rowan
Westminster Fibers
4 Townsend West
Suite 8
Nashua, NH 03064
tel: 603-886-5841
www.knitrowan.com

Blue Sky Alpacas
Bulky Alpaca

A super-bulky-weight wool-blend yarn
Recommended knitting needles: size 15 (10mm)
Gauge: 7 sts x 11 rows per 4" (10cm) over St st
Ball size: 45yd/41m per 3½ oz/100g ball
Yarn specification: 50% alpaca, 50% wool

Debbie Bliss
Cashmerino Aran

A medium-weight (worsted-weight) wool-blend yarn
Recommended knitting needles: size 8 (5mm)
Gauge: 18 sts x 24 rows per 4" (10cm) over St st
Ball size: 98yd/90m per 1¾ oz/50g ball
Yarn specification: 55% merino wool, 33% microfiber, 12% cashmere

Debbie Bliss
Cashmerino Chunky

A bulky-weight wool-blend yarn
Recommended knitting needles: size 10½ (7mm)
Gauge: 14 sts x 20–21 rows per 4" (10cm) over St st
Ball size: 70yd/65m per 1¾ oz/50g ball
Yarn specification: 55% merino wool, 33% microfiber, 12% cashmere

Debbie Bliss
Cashmerino Superchunky

A bulky-weight wool-blend yarn
Recommended knitting needles: size 11 (7.5mm)
Gauge: 12 sts x 17 rows per 4" (10cm) over St st
Ball size: 82yd/75m per 3½ oz/100g ball

Yarn specification: 55% merino wool, 33% microfiber, 12% cashmere

Debbie Bliss
Donegal Chunky Tweed

A bulky-weight wool yarn
Recommended knitting needles: size 10½ (7mm)
Gauge: 12 sts x 18 rows per 4" (10cm) over St st
Ball size: 109yd/100m per 3½ oz/100g hank
Yarn specification: 100% wool

Lanaknits Hemp for Knitting
Allhemp6

A double-knitting-weight (lightweight) hemp yarn
Recommended knitting needles: size 5 (3.75mm)
Gauge: 22 sts x 28 rows per 4" (10cm) over St st
Skein size: 165yd/150m per 3½ oz/100g skein
Yarn specification: 100% hemp

Rowan
Big Wool

A super-bulky-weight wool yarn
Recommended knitting needles: size 19 (15mm)
Gauge: 7.5 sts x 10 rows per 4" (10cm) over St st
Ball size: 87yd/80m per 3½ oz/100g ball
Yarn specification: 100% merino wool

Rowan
Cocoon

A bulky-weight wool-blend yarn
Recommended knitting needles: size 10½ (7mm)
Gauge: 14 sts x 16 rows per 4" (10cm) over St st
Ball size: 126yd/115m per 3½ oz/100g ball
Yarn specification: 80% merino wool, 20% kid mohair

Rowan
Summer Tweed

A medium-weight (worsted-weight) silk-blend yarn
Recommended knitting needles: size 8 (5mm)
Gauge: 16 sts x 23 rows per 4" (10cm) over St st
Ball size: 118yd/108m per 1¾ oz/50g hank
Yarn specification: 70% silk, 30% cotton

Rowan
Tapestry

A double-knitting-weight (lightweight) wool-blend yarn
Recommended knitting needles: size 6 (4mm)

Gauge: 22 sts x 30 rows per 4" (10cm) over St st
Ball size: 131yd/120m per 1¾ oz/50g ball
Yarn specification: 70% wool, 30% soybean fiber

Rowan Classic (RYC)
Baby Alpaca DK

A double-knitting-weight (lightweight) wool yarn
Recommended knitting needles: size 6 (4mm)
Gauge: 22 sts x 30 rows per 4" (10cm) over St st
Ball size: 109yd/100m per 1¾ oz/50g ball
Yarn specification: 100% baby alpaca

Rowan Classic (RYC)
Bamboo Soft

A double-knitting-weight (lightweight) bamboo yarn
Recommended knitting needles: size 5 (3.75mm)
Gauge: 25 sts x 30 rows per 4" (10cm) over St st
Ball size: 112yd/102m per 1¾ oz/50g ball
Yarn specification: 100% bamboo

Rowan Classic (RYC)
Cashcotton 4-Ply

A super-fine-weight (fingering) cotton-and-wool-blend yarn
Recommended knitting needles: size 3 (3.25mm)
Gauge: 28 sts x 36 rows per 4" (10cm) over St st
Ball size: 197yd/180m per 1¾ oz/50g ball
Yarn specification: 35% cotton, 25% polyamide, 18% angora, 13% viscose, 9% cashmere

Rowan Classic (RYC)
Cashsoft Aran

A medium weight (worsted-weight) wool-blend yarn
Recommended knitting needles: size 7 (4.5mm)
Gauge: 19 sts x 25 rows per 4" (10cm) over St st
Ball size: 95yd/87m per 1¾ oz/50g ball
Yarn specification: 57% extra fine merino wool, 33% microfiber, 10% cashmere

Rowan Classic (RYC)
Cashsoft 4-Ply

A super-fine-weight (fingering) wool-blend yarn
Recommended knitting needles: size 3 (3.25mm)
Gauge: 28 sts x 36 rows per 4" (10cm) over St st
Ball size: 197yd/180m per 1¾ oz/50g ball
Yarn specification: 57% extra fine merino wool, 33% microfiber, 10% cashmere

twenty-five men and a dog...

Alex

Alwyn

Andy

Cabral

Cory

Emil

Harry

Ian

James

Jean-Marc

Kaz

Kenny

Khary

Leo

Lewis

Lucasz

Mac

Mark

Oliver

Pete

Peter

Phill

Richard

Simon

Tuan

and Rufus

Publisher's acknowledgments

The publisher would like to thank the following for loaning clothes and accessories: American Apparel, B-Used, Canali, Comme des Garçons, Converse, Cutler and Gross, Etro Collezione, Fray, Gap, Givenchy, Hartford, Kangol, Kris van Asche, Lacoste, Lilal, McQ, Neil Barrett, Nudie, Paul Smith, Paul Smith PS, Peachoo + Krejburg, Superfine, Thom Browne, Thomas Burberry, Uniqlo, Westwood Man, Wintle, YMC.

Author's acknowledgments

I would like to thank: all the "boys" who came along to be photographed, often revealing their inner selves to the unequaled Chris Terry, with exceptional results; Quadrille, an exemplary publisher of exacting style and insight, led by Alison Cathie, who continually exceeds all boundaries; Editorial Director and mentor, Jane O'Shea, whose vision, encouragement, style, and belief in me have nurtured my career as a craft author. Creative Director, Helen Lewis for her innovation and diligence in each new project we undertake, and for surpassing all my expectations in pulling this complex concept together. Lisa Pendreigh, project editor whose rigorous support, unfathomable patience, and inimitable professionalism is without equal, I just couldn't be without her. And wow! It has been a privilege to have the exceptional Chris Terry photograph this collection, his insightful style and relaxed professionalism has made this book. There is something about menswear that creates its own energy and team spirit, or maybe it's just great to hang out with the boys again. My immense thanks to Simon for his intuitive and inspirational styling, together with Jean-Marc's strong and authoritative style, which contributed enormously to the shoot. Huge thanks and appreciation for the contribution made by Sally Lee, my creative practitioner, for her unswerving support, enthusiasm, expertise, and friendship. And to Mary Potter and Christine Dilley for their superb handknitting skills. Heartfelt thanks, too, for Rosy Tucker and her diligence, patience, and meticulous hard work in checking all the patterns—invaluable and reassuring. Special thanks to Rowan, Debbie Bliss and Designer Yarns, Lana Hames of Lanaknits and Blue Sky Alpacas for, first of all, creating yarns of the highest quality and innovation, but invaluably for their generosity in contributing yarns and enthusiastic support for this book. And to my lovely daughter, Arabella for "rounding up" such gorgeous friends and to Ian, my best critic. Thank you both for always being there for me, and indeed here in this book.

Published in the United States by Potter Craft, an imprint of the Crown Publishing Group, a division of Random House, Inc., New York.
www.crownpublishing.com
www.pottercraft.com

POTTER CRAFT and colophon is a registered trademark of Random House, Inc.

Originally published in paperback in Great Britain by Quadrille Publishing Ltd, London, in 2008.

Library of Congress Cataloging-in-Publication Data is available upon request.
ISBN: 978-0-307-46049-3

Printed in Singapore

10 9 8 7 6 5 4 3 2 1

First American Edition

The author and publisher would like to thank the Craft Yarn Council of America for providing the yarn weight standards and accompanying icons used in this book. For more information, please visit www.yarnstandards.com.